Plate of Food
Cookbook

Mostly good…a little bit of naughty

Text by Laura Timbrook

Recipes by Paige Hansen & Laura Timbrook

Photography by Paige & Rich Hansen

On the cover: Braised Chicken Thighs (page 70,) Grilled Green Beans (page 46,) with figs and bleu cheese

Copyright © 2015 Ginger & Fennel LLC

All rights reserved. The content of this book is for general instruction only. Each person's physical, emotional, and spiritual condition is unique. The instruction in this book is not intended to replace or interrupt the reader's relationship with a physician or other professional. Please consult your doctor for matters pertaining to your specific health and diet. No part of this publication may be reproduced, distributed, or transmitted in any form or by any means, including photocopying, recording, or other electronic or mechanical methods, without the prior written permission of the publisher or author, except in the case of brief quotations embodied in critical reviews and certain other noncommercial uses permitted by copyright law. For permission requests, email gingernfennel@gmail.com
ISBN: 0692538704

CONTENTS

Acknowledgements

Introduction — v

1. Know Your Ingredients — 1
2. Brunch — 22
3. Pasta & Grains — 32
4. Vegetables — 42
5. Soup — 60
6. Poultry — 68
7. Meat — 76
8. Seafood — 84
9. Quick Bites — 90
10. Sauces — 98
11. Sweet Indulgence — 104
12. Gluten-Free Index — 114
13. Pantry List — 115
14. Common Substitutions — 116

ACKNOWLEDGEMENTS

Without the support of our friends and families, this book would not have been possible. From the endless food tests, book reviews, early hours, and missed workouts, you have provided constant support. To our husbands Trevor and Rich, thank you for believing in us and for your tireless support. A special thanks to Crossfit Advanced, Kula Heart Yoga, and Switchback Pizza Company for allowing us to hold events to show off our book.

INTRODUCTION

Have you ever meet someone who didn't want to be healthy?

Of course not. We all want to be healthy. However, figuring out how to be healthy often leaves us with questions. Do we eat carbs? Gluten? Animal proteins? Is kale really good for us?

As an integrative nutrition coach, and a chef, we often hear, "what do I eat?" or "I don't have the time to make that." Today, there is an abundance of often conflicting information on food and nutrition. We are inundated with fad diets, frozen meal plans, and supposedly "healthy" fast food.

Much of our food comes from large commercial farms, out of a box, a can, or from a drive-thru window. Food can nourish our body and soul. We should enjoy eating it, talking about it, and sharing it. Food can make us feel happy and healthy, or sad and sick. Following a few basic principles, we can lead a happy, healthy life.

Tips for leading a healthy diet

The 80/20 principle: "Mostly good, with a little bit of naughty." Eighty percent of the time eat good food full of nutrition. Exercise regularly, and get quality sleep. Twenty percent of the time forget the rules, and have fun. It is easier to lead a healthy life when we have balance.

Focus on real food: If it's made in a factory, leave it. If it comes from a farm, enjoy it. Farmer's markets, in our opinion should be a staple for anyone focused on real food. Not only are the fruits and veggies fresher and more nutritious, they also help support your local economy. You may try something new based on their recommendation, or find a new way to prepare your favorite vegetable. To find local farmer's markets and farms, check out these great resources:

www.localharvest.com
www.eatwild.com

Seasonal food: Eating with the seasons is not only better for our bodies, it is also more affordable. Enjoying blueberries at their peak in July will provide you with fresher, more nutritious berries. It will also likely cost half of what lower quality berries, from far away locations, do in the winter. Food also tastes better when it is in season.

We wrote this book to get back in touch with wholesome food, made with fresh ingredients, from local farms. To get back to simple, healthy ingredients, such as oregano, garlic, and ginger. We don't have to find exotic produce from the far reaches of the world to nourish ourselves. We need to regain the simple concept of a homemade Plate of Food.

1

KNOW YOUR INGREDIENTS

If we don't understand what we are eating, how can we truly know we are properly nourishing our body? Marketing is a huge element of the food industry. Did you know food manufacturers purposely place green labels on products, to give the impression of being healthy to the consumer? Instead of blindly trusting a label, we need to properly educate ourselves. Cooking more food from scratch gives you more control over the individual ingredients. We can take it one step further by understanding what ingredients we are putting in our food, and why. From there, we can make healthy informed choices.

Fats
It used to be all fat was considered bad, and that it was the main, if not only, reason we were fat. This simply isn't true. There are several good fats, and it's important to understand that good fats can help keep us healthy and strong.

How the body utilizes fat
- Energy storage.
- Carries essential nutrients such as Vitamin, A, D, E, and K through the body.
- Protects organs during trauma.
- Regulates body temperature.
- Our brains are approximately 60% fat.

With too much body fat, however, we can become overweight and unhealthy. Conversely, when we have too little fat, we become malnourished and unhealthy.

Omega-3, 6, and 9 fatty acids

Fatty acids are building blocks for cell membranes, and are required to properly regulate inflammation. In order for these fatty acids to work properly, it is important to maintain a balance between them. Omega-3 & 6 are found in polyunsaturated fats, and are known as "essential fatty acids" (they must be obtained through diet.) Omega-6 is responsible for inflammation in the body, which helps with blood clotting and immune response. Omega-3 is responsible for reducing inflammation in the body and is often found in whole foods, such as grass-fed animals, fresh wild fish, as well as, nuts and seeds. It is important to make sure to keep a balanced level of 3 & 6. Too much Omega-6 can lead to chronic inflammation in our body. Since it is easy to gather Omega-6 from our diet due to the abundance of inflammatory foods, it is important that we focus on consuming foods higher in Omega-3.

Omega-9 is found in monounsaturated fat is considered "non-essential"(our bodies can make it.) Omega 9 plays a role in the balancing of blood sugar, however since our bodies can make this on their own, it is not necessary to take in additional Omega-9 through supplements.

Saturated fat

A saturated fat is a fully saturated fat molecule, which provides a stable structure. Saturated fats are needed to help stabilize cell membranes, and protect from damage.
- Usually solid at room temperature, saturated fats grow softer in warmer temperatures.
- Best for cooking at high temperature, and has the longest shelf life.
- Coconut Oil.
- Butter/Ghee.
- Beef, pork, poultry, milk, and cheese.

Unsaturated fat

Monounsaturated fats

Liquid at room temperature, monounsaturated fats can begin to solidify when cooled. They have a shorter shelf life than saturated fats, but longer than polyunsaturated fats. Monounsaturated fats should be used only when cooking on a lower heat or in vinaigrettes.
- Olive oil.
- Avocado oil.
- Canola oil.
- Fish oil.

Polyunsaturated fats
- Very short shelf life.
- Becomes rancid quickly.
- Not generally recommend for cooking.
- Always remain in a liquid state.

    Polyunsaturated Omega-6's
    - Safflower oil.
    - Sunflower oil.
    - Sesame oil.
    - Grapeseed oil.

    Polyunsaturated Omega-3's
    - Fish oil.
    - Flaxseed.
    - Pumpkin seed.
    - Hemp seed.
    - Walnut seed.

Trans fats

Trans fats are a byproduct of a process called hydrogenation, which turns unsaturated fats into a solid to mimic a saturated fat. This process helps protects these oils from becoming rancid. Trans fats are often listed on labels as "partially hydrogenated oil."

- Increases inflammation.
- Increases LDL cholesterol ("bad" cholesterol.)
- Risk of hardening of the arteries.
- Should be completely avoided.

Recommended fats

Olive oil

- Monounsaturated fat
- Use extra-virgin cold pressed olive oil, as it is the most pure, and has not been denatured by a heating process.
- Look for recent harvest dates, this helps ensures the freshness of olive oil. A recently harvested, cheaper olive oil, may be better than an old, yet more expensive, olive oil.
- Best with lower cooking temperatures and in vinaigrettes.

    Health benefits
    - Contains antioxidants.
    - Helps lower LDL cholesterol ("bad" cholesterol.)
    - Has been shown to help lower blood pressure.

Coconut oil

- Medium chain fatty acid (MCT)
- Use virgin, or extra virgin, cold pressed coconut oil, as it is the most pure, and has not been denatured by a heating process.
- Good for cooking, especially higher heat.
- Great addition for smoothies. It provides additional fat, which helps keep you fuller longer, while providing energy (when adding into smoothies, it is best to liquefy first.)

    Health benefits
    - Since MCTs resemble more of a carbohydrate than a fat, they metabolize faster. Most fats have to wait for bile to break down, while MCTs go directly from the liver to the digestive tract to be used for energy.
    - Contains lauric acid, which helps fight viruses, bacteria, and fungus.
    - Helps you feel fuller longer, and can help curb overeating.
    - Raises HDL cholesterol ("good" cholesterol.)

Ghee (aka clarified butter)
- Healthy saturated fat, especially from grass-fed animals.
- Tastes great.
- Ghee is clarified butter, which means milk solids have been removed.
- Easy to make at home.

Those who are sensitive to either casein or lactose, may be able to tolerate ghee, as it is low in both due to clarification.

> Health benefits
> - Helps reduce inflammation.
> - Assists in digestive track healing.
> - Good source of vitamin A, D, E, and K.
> - High in conjugated linoleic acid (CLA) which has been shown to improve insulin resistance.

Nut/Seed oils
- Polyunsaturated fats.
- Best used for a vinaigrette or finishing oil.
- Can provide a variety of flavors, due to the different nut and seed types available. They are a great way to change up the flavor of a vinaigrette.
- Very short shelf life. Keep in cool dark places, like the refrigerator.
- Not recommended for cooking due to being polyunsaturated fats.

Conclusion

A few key oils on hand are all you really need. We generally only cook using olive oil, coconut oil, or butter. We also use a few nut oils for finishing recipes, or changing up a vinaigrette. When using high heat, choose ghee or coconut oil. When using medium heat, choose butter or olive oil. If baking, butter or coconut oil can replace vegetable oil.

Sugars & Sweeteners

Sugar is generally used as an immediate source of energy. What isn't used our body stores for the preservation of muscle. Few people take a balanced approach, and many fall into one of the following categories:

- Avoid it like the plague, and haven't eaten it in years.
- Avoid it for the most part, but when they do, it's a total binge fest.
- Emotional bingers. They can go without it for the most part, but when emotions run high…watch out donuts.
- Eat way too much, generally in the form of processed foods, drinks, and sugary sweets.

Sugar rules

- Focus on eating more fresh foods, and less on processed foods.
- If you are craving something sweet, make it yourself. This way, you can control the quality of ingredients, as well as, the amount of sugar. Sometimes, by the time you are done cooking, the craving may have subsided.
- Avoid soft drinks and artificial sweeteners. Artificial sweeteners give us a false sense of security that eating something sweet can be part of our regular diet with no weight gain. Artificial sweeteners have also been shown to shut down a hormone (GLP-1) that tells us we are full, thus it is easier to end up over eating.
- If using a sweetener, choose one that contains some vitamins, minerals, or other healthy properties, not just empty calories.

Forms of sugars and sweeteners

There are many sweeteners and different forms of sugar. Here are some of the more common types:

Granulated sugar

This is the most common of all sugars. So what's the difference between white, dark brown, light brown or raw (turbinado)? Basically, it is the quantity of minerals and molasses that are left in the sugar crystals after processing. For example, white sugar has been highly processed to remove minerals and molasses to make it white. It's all processed sugar, just some has a higher molasses content.

Honey

This is one form of sugar that packs some healthy benefits. The best form of honey to use is locally sourced, and in the raw. Raw honey has not been heated, and all the nutritional value is still present. Using honey that has been pasteurized (heated,) the nutritional value is gone, making it no better than processed sugar.

Maple syrup

Maple syrup comes from sap of a maple tree. It is harvested in late winter or early spring, and heated to make syrup. Maple syrup comes in different grades, depending on the color. The darker the syrup, the higher it is in antioxidants, and the richer it is as a source of minerals. When choosing maple syrup, we recommend Grade A Extra Dark.

Health benefits
- High in antioxidants.
- Rich source of thiamine, zinc, and manganese.
- Contains other minerals such as potassium, copper, selenium, and phosphorus.

Agave nectar

Initially, agave nectar was considered a healthy alternative, because it is relativity low on the glycemic index. This is because 90% of the nectar is fructose. Since fructose is not metabolized by the body well, the effect on blood sugar levels is minimal. While fructose doesn't have a drastic effect on blood sugar, is does have harmful effects on the liver, and can promote obesity. As a result, limiting the consumption of fructose, including Agave nectar, is recommended.

High fructose corn syrup (HFCS)

This is not a natural form of sugar, it is an industrialized sweetener. Cane sugar is a 50/50 ratio of fructose/glucose, and is tightly bonded. HFCS has a 55/45 ratio and is unbound. While the ratio is close, your body doesn't break it down in the same manner, due to the unbound properties. A study done at Duke University, found that a higher consumption of HFCS was associated scaring of the liver.

Artificial sweeteners

These are chemical substances that taste sweet, but have no effect on blood sugar or caloric intake. In a sense they seem great, they taste good, and have no calories. We were always taught "if something is too good to be true, it probably is," and artificial sweeteners are no different. Artificial sweeteners have several nasty side effects:

- They trick your body into thinking it needs to metabolize sugar. When our taste buds sense something sweet, this triggers our pancreas to create insulin. The insulin, once produced, waits for the sugar to enter the blood stream. When sugar does not enter the blood stream, the body reabsorbs the insulin. Over time, the body stops producing the amount of needed insulin. This leads to blood sugar issues, when insulin is actually needed.
- Have been shown to lead to additional weight gain, due to both over eating caused by the GLP1 hormone being shut down, and because they slow down the metabolism.
- Linked to cardiovascular disease, diabetes, and obesity.

Conclusion

As a society in general, we consume too much sugar. On average, a person consumes 150-170 lbs. of sugar a year. Sugar in moderation is fine, we just recommend using a natural form of sugar when doing so. Our favorite go to sweeteners are raw honey, and maple syrup. We find these best to use when cooking or baking smaller family size batches to enjoy for a quick dessert. When cooking or baking larger portions, for a party or event, we stick with conventional sugar, and just remember balance and moderation.

Grains

It seems as though being "grain-free," or "gluten-free," is a dietary trend right now. Many grains, both gluten, and gluten-free, contain health benefits. Grains often are high in fiber, vitamins, and minerals. However, some individuals may do best to avoid them for a period of time due to health issues, if recommend by their healthcare professional.

What is Gluten

Gluten is the protein in wheat. While people have been avoiding gluten like the plague, we recommend a more balanced approach:

- Enjoy gluten in moderation: bagels, pizza, pretzels, and pasta contain the highest amount.
- If you have been diagnosed with an allergy to gluten, avoid it.
    - Read all labels: condiments, makeup and many personal care products (such as shampoo) often contain gluten.
- If you have a sensitivity to, or feel better when not consuming gluten, stay away. Focus on healing your gut with fresh fruits and veggie, fermented foods, and good quality lean protein. Many times, once your gut is healed, gluten can be slowly reintroduced. It is recommended to work with your healthcare professional in healing the gut.
- Try sourdough products: the fermentation process helps breaks down gluten and makes it more digestible.
- Many times, dishes that call for noodles can easily be substituted with zucchini noodles or spaghetti squash.
- Remember, gluten-free doesn't equal healthy, a cookie is still a cookie even if it is gluten-free.
- Many gluten-free bread products contain a high amount of yeast. This can cause just as many problems for someone with a digestive issue. If you do better eating gluten-free, stick to a whole-foods gluten-free diet, and avoid prepackaged foods.

If you find that you are sensitive to gluten, I recommend working with your healthcare professional to determine if it's all gluten or just certain varieties. I have seen clients that are sensitive to highly processed grains, such as store-bought bread, but can handle sour-leavened bread fine. I have also seen clients that cannot eat pasta, but can eat farro. Keep in mind everyone is different, so what works for one might not be the same for you.

Ancient grains

This term is used to describe some hearty, nutrient-dense, grains and seeds with ancient origin. These grains are a powerhouse for nutrients, containing protein and serving as rich sources of vitamins and minerals. Often, these grains have been referenced in ancient cultures and scriptures.

"Ancient grains" commonly include: amaranth, spelt, farro, kamut, millet, quinoa, sorghum, teff, freekeh, and chia.

Types of grains

Quinoa
Considered sacred by the Inca, and pronounced [KEEN-wah], quinoa is considered a grain, but technically it is a seed. Quinoa contains no gluten, so it can be useful for those with sensitivities.

Health benefits
- High in protein.
- Considered a complete protein, which means it contains all essential amino acids.
- Gluten-free.
- Higher in fiber than most grains.
- High in vitamins and minerals such as iron, lysine, magnesium, riboflavin (B2) and manganese.

Bulgar wheat
The whole form of wheat, this means it does contain gluten. Those who are sensitive to gluten should avoid it.

Health benefits
- High in insoluble fiber, good for digestive health.
- Good source of B vitamins, such a niacin (B3), thiamine (B1), folate, and B6.

Oats
While oats are naturally gluten free, many are processed in wheat factories. Those with gluten sensitivity should look for oats that state "gluten-free."

Health benefits
- High in dietary fiber.
- Good source of vitamin B and magnesium.
- Due to the high fiber content, oats can work to help stabilize blood sugar.
- Contain Beta-Glucans that help boost immune system.

Couscous
This is a small grain-like pasta made out of semolina, a course whole wheat common in pasta. Couscous is often a favorite with kids, and is great when mixed with fresh veggies. Since semolina is a form of wheat, it is not a gluten-free grain.

Health benefits
- High in dietary fiber.
- Contains B vitamins such as thiamin, niacin, riboflavin, B6, folate, and pantothenic acid.
- Good source of protein: 1 cup = 6 grams of protein.

Farro

Common in Italian cooking, most of the Farro found today comes from Italy. It is comprised of 3 different wheat varieties: farro piccolo (einkorn,) farro medio (emmer,) and farro grande (spelt.) Most of what can be found in stores today is farro medio, the emmer wheat variety. Since Farro is a form of wheat, this grain does contain gluten.

Health Benefits
- High in fiber.
- Good source of B vitamins and magnesium.
- Contains 14 grams of protein per cup of raw farro.

Flax

One of the oldest cultivated seeds, with history dating back to 3000 BC. While whole flax seeds are great, be careful with ground flax seeds and flax oils. These seeds are very susceptible to heat, and tend to go rancid quickly. If you find yourself having digestive issues, try making a flax seed granola, and enjoying it for breakfast for a few days.

Health benefits
- High in fiber.
- High in omega-3's.
- Rich source of vitamins and minerals such as manganese, B1, and essential and fatty acids.
- Great for cardiovascular health.

Spelt

Spelt is a species of wheat believed to be about 9,000 years old. It can be found referenced in biblical scripture. While this form of wheat does contain gluten, it contains less than other forms of wheat.

Health benefits
- High in fiber.
- Complete protein, meaning it contains all the essential amino acids.
- More easily digested than other forms of wheat.
- 1 cup of spelt (raw) contains 25 grams of protein.
- Contains a phytonutrient, called lignans, which can help fight breast cancer.

Chia

Remember those chia pets that grew hair on the terra cotta planter? Yup, it's the same seed. Lately chia is making a huge comeback in the health and wellness field, from chia kombucha tea to chia seed ice pops. Chia is technically a seed, and when added to water, forms a gelatinous barrier around the seed.

Health benefits
- Great source of fiber, out of 12 grams of carbs, 11 of them are fiber.
- Gluten-free.
- High in protein, 4 grams per ounce.
- High in omega-3's.
- Have been shown to lower LDL cholesterol.
- High in manganese, phosphorus, and calcium.

Rice

Rice is a staple food in several cultures, and is great for providing quick, sustained energy. Rice comes in different varieties, brown rice to white rice, as well as, long, medium, and short grain varieties.

White rice vs. brown rice

The difference between these forms is that white rice has had the hull removed from the rice, while brown rice has the hull intact. Many consider the brown rice variety more nutritious because the hull remains intact, but that can make digestion more difficult for some. We recommend experimenting to see which one you feel best eating.

Long-grain: Considered "all-purpose" rice, as it does well in almost all forms of cooking. Specialty varieties of these are basmati and jasmine rice.

Medium-grain: Used most commonly in Japanese Sushi and Spanish Paella. Bomba is the preferred variety in Paella.

Short-grain: the most common form of short grain variety is the arborio rice which is commonly used in Italian cooking for making risotto.

Greens

It's no surprise that greens are healthy. However, as an integrative nutrition coach, it's too often I see many people try to go from iceberg lettuce to kale, but they end up not liking kale, and they go right back to iceberg. What they don't realize is that there are a ton of other greens, from sweet to savory, and from mild to strong, they can try. In this section we will be going over two major types of greens:

- Leaf lettuce.
- Dark leafy greens.

While each variety of greens contains a particular makeup of vitamins, a few vitamins and minerals remain consistent throughout. Each variety also adds a few additional nutrients and benefits to the list.

Health benefits
- Contains vitamins A, B, and K.
- Good for minerals such as: manganese, copper, magnesium, selenium, phosphorus, potassium, and iron.
- Contains fiber to keep you full, and aid in digestive health.

Leaf Lettuce

Iceberg: While it has some nutrition, iceberg has the smallest amount of nutrition among lettuces, however, it's still better than french fries.

Romaine: Found in Greek and Caesar salads, this lettuce has a good crunch, similar to iceberg, and has a mild flavor, good for those just getting used to eating more lettuce. Romaine is not only crunchy and mild tasting, but also packs some solid nutrients.

Health benefits
- Protein: Believe it or not, an entire head of romaine lettuce contains about 7 grams of protein and nine different amino acids.
- Beta-carotene: One head of romaine lettuce contains more beta carotene than a large carrot.
- Vitamin and minerals: High in vitamin B and K, as well as, minerals such as manganese, copper, magnesium, selenium, phosphorus, potassium, and iron.

Butterhead Lettuce

Often found in the store labeled as Butter, Boston, or Bibb lettuce, it is a bit more expensive than romaine, but definitely has its benefits. While not as crunchy as romaine, it has a nice mild, sweet, flavor that works amazing for bun less burgers.

Health Benefits
- High in vitamins A, B, and K.
- Good source of minerals such as, iron, magnesium, manganese, and phosphorus.

Red and Green Lettuce

Two of the most common lettuces, recognized by their loose leafs, red leaf lettuce will have red tops instead of solid green. Mild in flavor, these are a great all-purpose lettuce to have on hand.

Health benefits
- Good source of fiber, helps keep you fuller longer.
- 1 cup contains 70% of our recommended daily allowance of vitamin A.
- Contains vitamin K, which helps prevent hardening of the arteries.

Radicchio

Hearty red leaves with a white spine, these create good lettuce cups to fill with your favorite salads or meats. They also make a great shell for tortilla-less tacos. Since this lettuce can be slightly bitter, is it perfect for a filling or salad that contains fruit or meat with a more prominent flavor that can complement the flavor of the radicchio.

Health benefits
- Great for the digestive system.
- High in vitamins A, B, and K, as well as, many minerals.
- Contains a component call inulin that helps regulate blood sugar.
- High in dietary fiber, which helps fight LDL cholesterol.
- Good source of antioxidants.

Endive

Endive, like radicchio, is great for making cups for serving meat salads. They are the light white/yellow, and have thin shaped heads. We love these for brunch, especially when plated as boats with radicchio, and kids love when food can resemble a toy boat!

Health benefits
- High in vitamins A, K, and B.
- Good source of manganese which helps in the regulation of blood sugar and metabolism.
- Contains kaempferol, a flavonoid that can help reduce the risks of some cancer.

Dark Leafy Greens

When most people think of dark leafy greens, they think particularly of kale, the curly lettuce that has traditionally been used on catering trays as a garnish. Dark leafy greens have amazing health benefits, and each one has a slightly different texture and flavor. Some are great in salads, while others are best in stir fries, or mixed with fruit. Like most greens, the smaller the variety (baby or micro,) the more tender and sweet they will be.

Spinach

Probably the tastiest of the dark leafy varieties, I have found most clients like spinach. From there, we can work our way up the other dark leafy green varietals. I strongly recommend, if adding dark leafy greens to your diet, to start with spinach.

Swiss chard

Most notable for its rainbow stem, it is the highlight of just about any farm stand in the spring. The colors can range from deep red to vibrant yellow. Swiss chard has a great mild taste, and a texture that is a bit firmer than spinach, but not as hearty as kale.

Health benefits
- High in antioxidants that help fight cancer, and keep us looking young.
- Good source of vitamin A, C, and K, as well as, minerals such as iron, magnesium, and potassium.
- One of the highest foods in vitamin K
- Great for bone and blood health, due to its vitamin and mineral profile.
- High in dietary fiber which can help regulate weight.

Beet Greens

These are the greens that are attached to the beet root that so many of us are used to eating. The vitamin K in beet greens have also been shown to help prevent osteoporosis, and may help in the fight against Alzheimer's disease.

Health benefits
- One cup of cooked beet greens contains 4 grams of protein.
- Good source of fiber, phosphorus, and zinc.
- Packed with antioxidants.
- High in vitamin B6, copper, magnesium, manganese, and potassium.
- Even higher in iron than spinach.
- Has a better nutritional profile than the beet root.
- Vitamin K has healthy blood clotting properties.
- Vitamin A helps boost the immune system.

Collards

If kale and cabbage had a baby, collards would be it. It has a similar nutritional profile to kale, however, it's sturdy, and tastes more like cabbage. I have found collards to be best when they have been slow cooked, which tenderizes the leaf, and mutes its cabbage-like taste.

Health benefits
- One of the highest sources of vitamin A and K.
- High in B vitamins: B-1, B-5, B-6, riboflavin, niacin, and folic acid,
- Good source of vitamin C.

Kale

I have a confession to make: as an integrative nutrition coach, I feel as though I need to be eating kale like it is second nature, and is the answer to all my prayers. Honestly, though, I have to say I haven't been a big fan. I used to add it in salads as a baby variety since it isn't as bitter, and I do love kale chips. Paige made me the kale and peach salad (page 58,) and I loved it. If you are like me, here are a few pointers when dealing with kale to start your love affair:

- Baby and micro versions are the sweetest. Smaller = tender and sweet.
- Kale from a local farm or farmer's market, and kale from a supermarket, are vastly different. The supermarket produce is often older, tougher, and bitter, while kale from a farmer's market will likely be on the tender, and sweeter side.
- Kale is great mixed in a salad with fruit, as the sweetness of the fruit cuts the bitter properties of the kale.
- I have yet to meet a kid who doesn't like kale chips (page 59.)
- Kale mixed with pineapple in smoothies is virtually undetectable.
- Kale has so many health benefits it really is worth finding the ways you like it the best.

Health benefits
- Considered to be one of the most nutritious foods on the planet.
- Good source of vitamin C.
- High in vitamins A, K, B, calcium, copper, magnesium, manganese, and potassium.
- Has been shown to lower cholesterol.
- One of the highest sources of vitamin A and K.
- High in lutein, which can help protect eyes.

Roots, Herbs, and other Notable foods

Traditional medicine has been using roots, herbs, spices, and fruits for eons for healing. Some have been significantly researched, and provide some amazing health benefits. A few of my favorites:

Lemon

Lemons are at the top of my list of favorite ingredients. They can brighten salads, or fish, help detox the body, and make water taste great. Due to the numerous health benefits of lemons, I recommend clients drink a cup of warm lemon water upon waking.

Health benefits
- The great detoxifier: good for the liver, bile, and digestion.
- Aids in fat metabolism.
- Lemons are also high in vitamin C. I recommend clients drink warm lemon water upon waking to help with the cleansing and digestion process.
- Lemons help balance the ph levels of the body.

Ginger

If I had to choose a favorite ingredient, ginger would be it. Ginger can add an exotic flavor to a meal or dessert. It can give lemon water a whole new flavor, and contains great health and healing benefits. Ginger has been used in traditional healing, particularly in Chinese and Ayurvedic medicine. In Ayurvedic medicine, ginger is called "Vishvabheshaja," which means "universal remedy."

Health benefits
- Soothes upset stomachs.
- Improves digestion ability, and aids in intestinal gas relief.
- A study published in the *Journal of Agriculture Technology* in 2001 found that ginger can help treat foodborne illnesses.
- Ginger has been found helpful for various conditions, such as: constipation, nausea, ulcers, arthritis, diabetes, and cancer.
- Helps lower LDL cholesterol.

Turmeric

There is no such thing as a true miracle pill, however, in my opinion, turmeric is the closest thing. I was recently giving a healing food seminar at a corporation in which we discussed turmeric. Afterward, I spoke with a woman who told me that where she previously lived in India, wounds would be packed with turmeric, and then wrapped to prevent infection and aid healing.

Health benefits
- Active compound called curcumin, which is effective in relieving inflammation.
- Aids in liver and gallbladder function, which help break down fats.
- In Ayurveda, turmeric decreases congestion from mucous, helping digestive disorders.
- Helps in eliminating menstrual cramps due to its antispasmodic properties.
- In a 2011 study by the Department of Pharmacology, Government Medical College, turmeric was shown as a potential treatment for depression.

Parsley

With a solid vitamin, mineral, enzyme, and antioxidant profile, this herb is much more than just a simple garnish. I put parsley in just about everything I cook. For one, I love seeing the green color on a plate, in eggs, or sauces, but it also gives a very clean flavor to a dish.

Health benefits
- Freshens breath: chlorophyll that gives it the green color helps neutralize odors, and freshens breath.
- High content of flavonoids, limonene, and chlorophyll which aids the body in purifying the blood, and regeneration of tissue.
- Good for your eyes. Parsley contains lutein, and zeaxanthin, along with beta-carotene, which aid in eye health.
- High amount of vitamin K keeps bones healthy.
- Contains eugenol, which helps regulate blood glucose levels.
- Juice of parsley helps cleanse liver, and kidneys.

Oregano

Not just for Italian food, I might use more oregano than salt. Surprisingly, oregano is also a hearty herb, it grows well in a planter, and is easily moved indoors during cooler months. A good way to change up scrambled eggs is to add fresh oregano and parsley.

Health benefits
- High in antioxidants, with four times as many as blueberries.
- The anti-parasitic properties of oregano oil are often used to kill intestinal parasites.
- Oil of oregano can be an effective treatment in candida overgrowth.
- Helps reduce inflammation, and aids in overall joint health.

Garlic

In our family, we use garlic for cooking, but also for ear infections, and common colds. When my kids were small, every time they were teething they got ear infections. Our pediatrician recommended garlic ear oil, and after that, they almost never got an ear infection. Since the ear, nose, and throat are interconnected, at the first sign of colds or sickness, ear drops go in, and then they very rarely get sick.

Health benefits
- Helps lower LDL cholesterol.
- Fights intestinal parasites due to anti-parasitic properties.
- Antiviral and anti-bacterial to help keep you healthy.
- Allicin, a compound in garlic was shown to fight drug-resistant bacteria in a 2004 study from University of East London's School of Health and Biosciences.

Vitamins and Minerals

I always stress to my clients we first nourish with food and then use supplements, if needed. Nutrients in their natural state often have the corresponding enzymes needed to utilize and break them down, thus keeping a proper balance. Taking supplements, however, when not taking the correct formulation or balance, can do more harm than good. A great example is calcium. For calcium to work properly, there needs to be a balance of magnesium, phosphorus, and vitamin D. Without enough vitamin D, your body can't utilize the calcium, and having too much phosphorus can actually leach calcium out of your body.

Basic Vitamins

Vitamin A (Retinol)
- First vitamin named, thus the name vitamin A.
- Part of the carotenoid family, it is often recognized by its orange color.
- Required for the formulation of rhodopsin, which helps us see better at night
- Aids in growth and healing of cells, which helps keep skin and bones healthy.
- Maintains the structural integrity of cells, and can be helpful preventing cancer.
- First symptom of vitamin A deficiency is normally issues seeing at night, or dry, red eyes.
- Dry bumpy skin on the backs of arms, known as "chicken skin," is also another sign of vitamin A deficiency.
- Fresh fruits and veggies are the best sources of vitamin A.
- Beta-carotene will either convert to vitamin A or acts as an antioxidant.

Thiamin, B1
- Metabolizes glucose for cellular energy.
- Assists in the conversion fat for energy and storage.
- Helps nerve, heart, and muscle functions.
- Good for overall heart health.
- Has been used to aid in healing from dental surgery.
- Deficiency in thiamin can cause muscle loss.

Riboflavin, B2
- Gives B vitamin the bright yellow color.
- Aids in the metabolism of carbs and fats.
- Helpful in maintaining good vision, and healthy hair, skin and nails.
- Those deficient in B2 often have cracks at the corners of mouth.

Niacin, B3
- Helps stimulate circulation.
- Aids in the break down and utilization of proteins, fats, and carbohydrates.
- Helps increase energy through utilization of food.
- Aids digestion.
- Helps to regulate blood sugar and blood pressure, and lowers cholesterol serum levels.
- Can be helpful in treating vertigo, leg cramps, and migraine headaches.

Pantothenic Acid, B5
- Most commonly found in mold, yeasts, plants, and animal products.
- Known as an anti-stress vitamin.
- Supports adrenal functions.
- Helps reduce the toxic effects on the body from antibiotics.
- Aids in the metabolism of carbohydrates, and fats, for the release of energy.
- Helps relieve fatigue induced by stress.
- Can assist with allergies, headaches, arthritis, and insomnia.

Pyridoxine, B6
- Assists in the metabolism, and transportation of, amino acids.
- Aids the utilization of food sources to energy, and release of glycogen from the liver.
- Helps with fluid balance, and electrical functions of the heart, nerves, and muscles.
- Helps maintain cellular magnesium levels.
- Minimizes premenstrual symptoms, and water retention.
- Generally, if estrogen levels are raised, more B6 is required.
- Can be helpful with skin problems such as acne, eczema, and dandruff.

Biotin, B7
- Aids in the metabolism of fats needed for the synthesis of fatty acids.
- Helps maintain healthy skin and hair, and may help with graying of hair, if associated with biotin deficiency.
- Has been used in diabetic patients to reduce blood sugar.
- Helps thyroid cancer patients' hair grow back.

Folate, B9
- Mostly found in dark leafy greens. For maximum benefit, the greens should be eaten raw, as folic acid is not heat-stable.
- Was initially used to cure anemia in pregnancy.
- Works closely with B12 to assist with iron availability in red blood cells.
- Aids in the production of red blood cells.
- Helps in the breakdown of proteins, and assists in amino acid conversion.
- Plays a critical role in the development and function of the nervous system and brain.
- Folic acid is the synthetic compound of folate.

Vitamin B12
- Mostly found in animal proteins, however, small amounts are found in fermented foods.
- Essential for metabolism, and the entire nervous system.
- Aids other vitamins and minerals in the formation of red blood cells.
- Known as the energy vitamin, it stimulates the body's utilization of fats, proteins, and carbohydrates.
- Along with folate, B12 can help with anemia

Vitamin C (Ascorbic Acid)
- Found in fruits and vegetables. Raw fruits and vegetables have the highest concentration.
- Helps prevent and treat the common cold, flu, and cancer by boosting immune system.
- Aids in the formation of collagen, which keeps connective tissue healthy.
- Aids in the metabolism of vitamins and amino acids for release of serotonin.
- Helps adrenal and thyroid function.

Vitamin D
- Regulates calcium metabolism, and the usage of phosphorus.
- For ideal bone health, calcium, magnesium, and vitamin D are required together.
- Vitamin D can help prevent diabetes, arthritis, high blood pressure, and heart attacks.
- Deficiency in vitamin D can cause excessive thirst, digestive issues, lack of energy, and headaches.

Vitamin E
- Primary job is to stabilize blood fats, so that they are protected from free radicals.
- Protects the adrenal and pituitary glands from oxidation.
- Protects eyes and skin from tissue damage.
- Required for fertility.

Vitamin K
- Helps blood clotting and coagulation.
- Assists in bone building.
- Should not be taken in supplement form unless under care of a physician.
- Those on blood clotting medications should speak to their physician before changing their diet, including veggies containing vitamin K.
- Increased vitamin K can affect blood thinner medication, if you are taking blood thinner medication, please consult your healthcare professional.

Vitamin L
- Most commonly found in hugs, kisses and cuddles from friends, children, spouse, and pets.
- Can be transferred into food by the home cook, or baker.
- Emotional vitamin and essential for overall health and happiness.
- Vitamin L has been known to cure frowns and tears.

Basic Minerals

Calcium
- Found in foods such as milk, yogurt, cheese, sardines, dark leafy greens, beans, nuts, and seeds.
- Almost all calcium stored in the body is in the bones.
- Maintaining a balanced level of calcium is critical for cardiac function.
- Calcium relies on a balance of other vitamins and minerals to work properly within the body, such as vitamin D, magnesium and phosphorus.

Iron
- Found in foods such as liver, beef, beans, dark leafy greens, egg yolks, and prunes.
- Primary function is the production of hemoglobin that carries oxygen to red blood cells.
- It is essential for premenopausal women to keep a balanced iron level, due to monthly blood loss.
- Vitamin C assists in the absorption of iron.
- Assists with energy level, and memory function.

Iodine
- Found in foods such as sea vegetables, fish, shellfish, Celtic or Himalayan salts, onions, mushrooms, green peppers, and spinach.
- Goiter, an enlargement of the thyroid, happens when iodine is insufficient.
- Critical in the bodies' hormone functions.
- Without proper thyroid function, there are effects on metabolism, energy, cholesterol synthesis, nerve and bone formation, as well as, healthy skin and nails.

Manganese
- Found in sprouted grains, beans, nuts, seeds, and greens.
- Essential mineral for enzyme function, affecting energy production, protein metabolism, and bone formation.
- A large amount of calcium will disrupt manganese absorption, while too much manganese can cause iron deficiency.
- Activates the enzyme needed to utilize biotin, B1, and vitamin C.
- Helps prevent osteoporosis.
- Assists in balancing hormones.

Magnesium
- Found in foods such as dark leafy greens, nuts, seeds, beans, grains, avocado, and apricots.
- Naturally relaxes muscles and digestive tract.
- Important for heart and blood pressure function.
- Required to balance calcium, phosphorus, and potassium within the body.
- Helps in the metabolism of proteins and carbohydrates.
- Can also help relieve PMS symptoms, and improves sleep.

Phosphorus
- Found in foods such as yogurt, salmon, meat, milk, cheese, seeds, lentils, and brewer's yeast.
- A diet too high in phosphorus can leach calcium from the body.
- Helps the formation of teeth and bones.
- Vital to energy production.
- Plays an important role in the utilization of carbohydrates, fats, and protein synthesis for muscle growth and repair.

Potassium
- Found in foods such as avocado, spinach, sweet potato, yogurt, banana, and apricots.
- Works with sodium to keep the body properly hydrated.
- For overall electrical function, potassium, calcium, phosphorus, magnesium, and sodium need to be properly balanced.
- Proper potassium is needed for overall sustained energy.
- Plays an important role in regulating blood pressure.
- Aids in conversion of proteins to amino acids, and in the carbohydrate breakdown of glucose to glycogen metabolism.

Selenium
- Found in foods like Brazil nuts, yellowfin tuna, halibut, grass-fed beef, sardines, liver, eggs, and spinach.
- Protects cells from oxidation in conjunction with gluthithione, and vitamin E.
- Helps regulate metabolism, and helps recycle vitamin C within the body.
- Aids in the support of the thyroid and immune system.

Zinc
- Found in oysters, grass-fed beef, yogurt, lamb, garbanzo beans, cashews, mushrooms, and spinach.
- Helps the metabolism of carbohydrates, and the synthesis of DNA.
- Needed in more than 100 enzymes for tissue building, the immune system, metabolic functions, and detoxification.
- Assists in wound healing, and boosts immune system.
- Plays a key role in male reproductive health.
- Helps keep eyes healthy, as it is needed to convert vitamin A.

2

BRUNCH

Chia Seed Pudding	25
Banana Bread	26
Spinach Mushroom Frittata	27
Spelt & Coconut Pancakes	28
Fruit Kabobs	29
Apple Tart	30
Cheddar Bacon Biscuits	31

Cheddar Bacon Biscuits

Fruit Kabobs

Chia Seed Pudding

Chia Seed Pudding

Chia seeds are a fantastic source of protein, vitamins, and minerals. Just one ounce of chia seeds contains 11 grams of fiber, and 4 grams of protein. Combing chia with coconut milk gives the nutrients the fat it needs to be absorbed by the body, and to be used as energy. This is a perfect breakfast for someone looking to be both gluten-free, and dairy-free. This also makes a wonderful healthy dessert or snack.

Makes: 4 servings

Ingredients
- ½ cup chia seeds
- 1 can coconut milk (full fat)
- 1 cup strawberries, pureed
- ½ teaspoon vanilla
- 1 fresh lime, juiced (1½ - 2 tablespoons)
- 1 teaspoon fresh basil, chopped
- 2 tablespoons pure maple syrup or raw honey
- pinch of kosher salt

Directions
Combine all ingredients into a bowl and stir well until combined. Use a whisk to break up coconut milk.
Pour into individual ramekins or bowls.
Refrigerate for 4 hours or until firm.
Serve chilled.

Chef's note:
Try these flavor alternatives: omit strawberry, lime, and basil. Replace with one of the following:

Chocolate: add ⅓ cup raw cacao powder.
Spiced: add in ¼ teaspoon ground cinnamon, pinch of cardamom, nutmeg, and clove.
Pumpkin Spiced: add 1½ teaspoon spices from chai spice mix (page 30,) and 2 tablespoons pureed pumpkin.

Banana Bread

A great way to use up those brown bananas. In 2009, a Japanese study was published in an issue of *Food Science and Technology Research* finding that brown spots on bananas can breakdown abnormal cells and boost our body's immune system. Since this bread isn't very sweet, it is perfect to serve for a dessert or brunch alongside some fruit, nuts, or yogurt.

Makes: 1 loaf pan

Ingredients
- 1 cup mashed overripe bananas (2-3 bananas)
- ⅔ cup granulated sugar
- ¼ cup unsalted butter, melted
- ½ teaspoon vanilla extract
- 2 large eggs
- 1¾ cup all-purpose flour
- ¾ teaspoon baking soda
- ½ teaspoon kosher salt

Directions
Preheat oven to 350°F.
Beat banana, vanilla, sugar, and butter in mixer.
Add in eggs one at a time, and beat.
In a separate bowl, combine flour, baking soda, salt, and mix.
In the flour mixture, make a well, pour in banana mixture, and fold until combined.
Butter a loaf pan, and pour in mixture. Bake for 40 minutes, or until a toothpick inserted comes out clean.

Spinach Mushroom Frittata

Veggies are often left out at breakfast. However, to get the proper amount of veggies in a day, we should be consuming veggies in all our meals. Omelets, scrambles, and frittatas are excellent in providing the veggies, protein, and fats, our bodies need to start off our day. Eggs, mushrooms, cheese, and spinach, all contain protein, as well as, additional essential vitamins and minerals.

Makes: 6 servings

Ingredients
- 2 tablespoons extra-virgin olive oil or unsalted butter
- 1 small white or yellow onion, diced
- 8 ounces mushrooms, thinly sliced (crimini, oyster, or shiitake)
- 1 pound fresh spinach (will yield 1 cup cooked)
- 12 large eggs
- ½ cup full fat coconut milk or heavy cream
- ¾ cup shredded gruyere cheese, divided
- ¼ teaspoon kosher salt
- ¼ teaspoon fresh ground black pepper

Directions
Place a rack in upper third of oven; preheat to 350°F.
Heat 1 tablespoon oil in a 10-inch nonstick ovenproof skillet over medium heat.
Add onion and mushrooms. Cook, stirring often, until softened, about 5 minutes.
Add spinach to wilt, drain excess liquid.
Meanwhile, in a large bowl, whisk eggs, and milk. Mix in ½ cup cheese. Season with salt and pepper.
Increase the heat to medium-high and add remaining 1 tablespoon oil to the skillet. Pour the egg mixture over the mushrooms and spinach, shaking the pan to evenly distribute mixture. Cook the frittata, without stirring, until its edges begin to set, about 5 minutes.
Sprinkle remaining ¼ cup cheese over eggs and transfer skillet to oven. Bake frittata until golden brown and center is set, 20-25 minutes.

Chef's Note:
Cast iron pan, or a deep pie plate can be used. Frittatas are a great way to use leftover ingredients. If substituting, make sure ingredients are cooked before adding them to the frittata.

Spelt & Coconut Pancakes

Traditional pancakes use white flour, which has limited nutrients and fiber. Spelt, being an ancient grain, contains significantly more nutrition, fiber, protein, as well as, essential vitamins and minerals. Coconut flour is also a powerhouse in fiber, combining these flours can be beneficial to the gut. Using mineral based salts and raw honey also help boost our mineral absorption and immune health.

Makes: 8 pancakes

Ingredients
- 1 cup spelt flour
- ¾ cup whole wheat flour
- ¼ cup coconut flour
- 4 teaspoons baking powder
- ¼ teaspoon cinnamon
- ½ teaspoon Himalayan salt
- 2 large eggs, beaten
- 2 tablespoons raw honey
- 1¾ cup raw milk
- ¼ cup coconut oil, melted

Directions
In a bowl, combine all dry ingredients, and mix thoroughly.
In a separate bowl, add all wet ingredients and mix.
In the dry ingredient bowl, create a well in the center to pour in wet ingredients.
Mix everything together. Do not over mix, there will be lumps.
Spoon batter onto hot, buttered cast-iron skillet.
When batter bubbles, flip over.
Repeat for remaining pancakes.
Top with fresh butter and pure maple syrup, or one of the toppings below.

Chef's note:
Try these alternate flavors or toppings:

Spiced Nut Pancake: add ½ cup toasted walnuts, chopped, and ¼ teaspoon ground nutmeg.
Banana: add ½ cup bananas, chopped, and ½ teaspoon vanilla extract.
Blueberry lemon: add ½ cup blueberries and 1 teaspoon lemon zest and 1 teaspoon lemon juice.
Fruit & Nut: add fresh berries, apples, or bananas, and top with toasted walnuts.
Yogurt: top with fresh vanilla or plain yogurt.
Honey: drizzle with raw honey.

Fruit Kabobs

Food is always more fun on a stick, or so my kids tell me. We love making these for the kids to munch on, and they are also a great alternative to the typical fruit platter. Adding more fruit and veggies into our diet can help control sweet cravings. You can get creative and do a fruit and veggie kabob, or drizzle with a little mineral based salt, or chocolate. Sprinkling with mineral based salt is a great way to assist with hydration and electrolyte balance on a hot summer's day, or during a sporting event.

Makes: 4 servings

Ingredients
- 8 pineapple pieces
- 8 whole strawberries
- 12 grapes
- 16 bite size pieces of seasonal fruit
- 4 skewers
- ½ cup bittersweet chocolate (60% cacao) (optional)
- 1 teaspoon coconut oil (optional)
- Celtic sea salt (optional)

Directions
Skewer fruit alternating, between fruit types.
Place chocolate and coconut oil in a bowl and place over a pot of simmering water to melt. or Drizzle the chocolate over all of the fruit, lightly sprinkle with salt, and serve.

Chef's note:
This is great to get kids involved in helping make food. You can use this with any fruits or raw veggies they want. Another great way to get the kids involved is to allow them to choose the fruits and veggies from the farm, or farmer's market.

Apple Tart

Store bought apple pastries are almost always full of sugar. Many times they also have high fructose corn syrup and coloring. This yummy apple tart offers fresh apples with a chai spice mix that helps to lower inflammation, improve digestion, boost the immune system, and balance blood sugar. Lower in sugar, it's a perfect way to satisfy a sweet tooth.

Makes: 4-6 servings

Ingredients

- 1 whole sheet puffed pastry, thawed, cut in thirds
- 3 whole apples, peeled, cored, halved, and sliced
- ¼ cup unsalted butter
- 2 tablespoons pure maple syrup
- 1 tablespoons chai spice mix, see below
- Vanilla bean ice cream, for serving (optional)

Chai Spice Mix
- 2 tablespoons ground cinnamon
- 2 tablespoons ground cardamom
- 2 teaspoons ground ginger
- 2 teaspoons Chinese five-spice powder
- 1 large nutmeg, grated
- 1 teaspoon fresh ground black pepper

Directions

Preheat the oven to 400°F.
Place the puffed pastry rectangles onto a baking pan lined with parchment paper.
In a small pan, melt butter, and add maple syrup.
Using a pastry brush, spread a thin layer of the melted maple butter on the puff pastry.
In a mixing bowl, combine apples, chai spice mix, and melted maple butter.
Arrange the apple slices, overlapping them on the pastry rectangles in a straight line.
Bake until the pastry is puffed and golden brown, about 20 minutes.
Remove from the pan immediately, slice and serve warm with vanilla bean ice cream.

Cheddar Bacon Biscuits

So often, unhealthy recipes are altered to be "healthy" by reducing fat and sugar. The issue with this is that it makes us believe that these once unhealthy foods are now truly healthy. In turn, we eat more, or more often. It has also been shown that when fat is reduced, we tend to overeat as we lose that "full" feeling. Remember the 80/20 principle is key, and this recipes definitely falls into the 20%. Sometimes recipes just come down to being better than those on a box, this is certainly one of them. When indulging in one of these, remember to enjoying only one, and savor, as the flavor is amazing. Take the time to find the best ingredients, such as pastured bacon, along with butter and cheese from farmer's markets.

Makes: 8 biscuits

Ingredients
- 6 ounces bacon
- 2 cups all-purpose flour
- 1 tablespoon baking powder
- 1 teaspoon kosher salt
- 2 teaspoons granulated sugar
- ½ teaspoon fresh ground black pepper
- 1 stick cold unsalted butter, grated (refrigerate until needed)
- 1 cup shredded extra-sharp cheddar cheese
- 1 cup buttermilk

Directions
Preheat an oven to 425°F.
In an 11-inch oven proof pan, cook the bacon in the oven until crisp, about 11-12 minutes.
Transfer the bacon to a paper towel lined plate. Pour the remainder of the bacon fat into a glass dish.
Using a pastry brush, spread a tablespoon of bacon fat evenly over the pan bottom.
Finely chop the bacon, and set aside.
In a large bowl, whisk together the flour, baking powder, salt, sugar, and pepper. Using a pastry blender, or two knives, cut in the cold butter until pea-size crumbs form.
Stir in the cheese and bacon.
Stir in the buttermilk until the dough just comes together.
Transfer the dough to a floured work surface and roll out into a 9½ by 11-inch rectangle.
Fold the dough into thirds, rotate 90 degrees, and roll out into the same size rectangle.
Fold into thirds again, rotate 90 degrees, and roll out into a 6 by 8½-inch rectangle, about ¾ inch thick.
Using a floured 2-inch biscuit cutter, cut out biscuits and place in pan.
Gather the remaining dough pieces, reroll to ¾ inch thick, and cut out additional biscuits.
Brush the tops of the biscuits with some of the remaining bacon fat.
Bake the biscuits 20-22 minutes, or until golden brown and a toothpick inserted into the center comes out clean.

3

PASTA & GRAINS

Creamy Barley Risotto with Mushrooms & Spinach	35
Orecchiette with Peas & Sausage	36
Homemade Egg Noodles	37
Macaroni and Cheese	38
Moroccan Inspired Couscous	39
Soba Noodle Salad	40
Cherry Pistachio Quinoa Salad	41

Orecchiette with Peas & Sausage

Creamy Barley Risotto with Mushrooms & Spinach

Cherry Pistachio Quinoa Salad

Creamy Barley Risotto with Mushrooms & Spinach

Nutrient, protein, and fiber dense, this is a great dish that can easily become a full meal. Barley, mushrooms, and spinach are all great plant based protein sources. The flexibility of this dish is endless, which makes this a great go-to recipe.

Makes: 4 servings

Ingredients
- 16 ounces mixed mushrooms (cremini, oyster, and/or shiitake)
- 4 cups unsalted broth (bone, beef, or vegetable)
- 3 tablespoons extra-virgin olive oil
- 3 cloves garlic, minced
- 16 ounces fresh spinach
- 1½ teaspoons kosher salt, plus more to taste
- ¾ teaspoon fresh ground black pepper, plus more to taste
- 1 tablespoon unsalted butter
- 1½ cups yellow or white onion, diced
- 1 cup pearl barley
- 3 sprigs fresh thyme
- 1 bay leaf
- ½ cup dry white wine
- ½ cup Parmigiano Reggiano cheese, grated, plus more for garnish.

Directions
Brush the mushrooms with a barely damp paper towel. Cut mushrooms as follows: quarter cremini mushrooms, gently break apart oyster mushrooms, or remove stem from shitake mushrooms and slice caps.

In a Dutch oven, heat 1 tablespoon olive oil over medium-high heat. Add the mushrooms, ½ teaspoon salt, ¼ teaspoon pepper, and 1 clove minced garlic. Sauté until the mushrooms are brown, soft, and give up their liquid. With a slotted spoon, transfer the mushrooms to a small bowl and set aside.

Reduce heat to medium. Add butter, and remaining olive oil. Add the chopped onion, and cook, stirring often, until the onions soften, 3-5 minutes.

Add remaining garlic, salt and pepper, thyme, bay leaf, and the barley. Stir to coat. Cook for 2 minutes. Add the wine, stir and cook another 2 minutes.

Add 3 cups of the broth to the barley. Stir, reduce to low heat, cover, and simmer for 40 minutes. Remove lid, and stir occasionally over medium heat until the broth is absorbed, constant stirring isn't necessary. Continue adding the broth, ½ cup at a time, until it is all absorbed and the barley is creamy, but maintains a bit of chew, 10-15 minutes additional time.

Remove thyme stems and bay leaf. Stir in fresh spinach to wilt. Add ½ cup Parmigiano Reggiano cheese. Taste and adjust salt and pepper, as desired.

Ladle the barley into bowls. Then top with mushrooms and additional cheese.

Dietary alternatives
Gluten-free: Substitute quinoa for barley.
Vegetarian or dairy-free: Substitute olive oil for butter and omit cheese.

Orecchiette with Peas & Sausage

Sometimes the healthiest part of a meal is being good for the soul. Growing up in an Italian family, there is a special spot in my heart for pasta. The greatest part of this dish is that the lemon helps to lighten the pasta and sausage, while the peas add bulk to the dish, helping to limit the amount of pasta you eat. Add zucchini or eggplant to this dish, if desired. The more veggies, the better.

Makes: 4 servings

Ingredients
- 1 tablespoon extra-virgin olive oil, plus more for serving
- 2 slices day-old bread, torn into small pieces, or given a quick turn in a food processor
- 3 tablespoons kosher salt, plus more to taste
- 3 cups dried orecchiette pasta
- 4 sausage links of Italian sausage, casings removed (approximately 1 pound)
- 2 cups peas (fresh or frozen)
- 4 large garlic cloves, minced
- ½ teaspoon red pepper flakes
- 1 lemon, zested and juiced
- ½ cup Parmigiano Reggiano cheese, grated
- fresh ground black pepper, to taste
- pea shoots for garnish (optional)

Directions
In a frying pan, over medium-low heat, warm olive oil. Add the bread crumbs, and stir to coat the pieces with the olive oil. Season lightly with salt and cook, stirring often, until the bread is golden brown, about 5 minutes. Pour onto a plate and let cool.
Bring pasta water to a boil, add 3 tablespoons of kosher salt, add pasta. Stir well, and cook 1 minute less than al dente, per the pasta package directions.
Meanwhile, in the pan, over medium-low heat, add the sausage, garlic, red pepper, and cook, stirring and breaking up the sausage meat with a wooden spoon, until the sausage is browned, about 7 minutes. Season with salt.
When the pasta is ready, scoop out, and reserve 1-2 cups of the pasta cooking water.
Add pasta to the sausage pan, along with the lemon juice, and 1 cup of the pasta cooking water to deglaze the pan.
Add peas and cheese, stir and toss well, over medium heat for the final minute of cooking. Adjust the consistency, if needed, with some of the pasta cooking water.
If using peas shoots, toss with warm pasta, and then divide into serving bowls.
Garnish with additional cheese, bread crumbs, fresh ground black pepper, a drizzle of olive oil and serve.

Homemade Egg Noodles

There is just something comforting about homemade noodles. With this recipe, you control the ingredients. Given that the number of ingredients is limited, these are easier to digest than typical store bought noodles, which often have additional ingredients and preservatives. They can also be easily adjusted to be gluten-free by substituting rice flour for all-purpose flour.

Makes: 4 servings

Ingredients
- 2 large eggs
- 1 egg yolk
- 1½ cups all-purpose flour
- ½ teaspoon kosher salt

Directions
In a bowl, mix eggs (including the additional yolk,) and 1 cup flour and salt. It will be very sticky.
Generously flour the counter-top, and your hands.
Knead in the remaining ½ cup of flour. The dough should be dry enough to handle.
Cover, and let dough rest for at least 30 minutes.
Roll dough out very thin. Noodles will double in size when cooked.
Cut noodles to your desired shape and size. A pizza cutter works well for cutting noodles.
Cook noodles in boiling broth, or salted water for 5-6 minutes (or until tender.)

Macaroni & Cheese

Remember that 80/20 principal? This is definitely a 20%. It's a "good for the soul" dish, made with love, butter, cream, and real cheese. This is definitely a dish for sharing with friends and family. To help not devouring this dish the next day, I highly recommend dividing the leftovers among friends!

Makes: 8-10 servings

Ingredients
- 1 pound pasta (recommended: Barilla Cellentani)
- 16 ounces whole milk mozzarella, grated
- 8 ounces extra sharp cheddar, grated
- 8 ounces Colby Jack cheese, grated
- 3 tablespoons unsalted butter
- 3 tablespoons all-purpose flour
- 3 cups whole milk, room temperature
- 1 teaspoon Dijon mustard
- ½ -¾ cup panko bread crumbs
- 3 tablespoons kosher salt, plus more to taste
- fresh ground black pepper, to taste

Directions
Preheat oven to 425°F.
Bring pasta water to boil, add 3 tablespoons of kosher salt. Cook pasta 2 minutes less then al dente directions, per the pasta package directions.
Drain and put in greased 9x13 pan.
In separate pan, make roux (see Chef's note below,) with butter and flour. Slowly add 1 cup of milk at a time, while whisking, to prevent lumps.
Add Dijon mustard. Add grated cheese, one cup at a time, stirring occasionally. Reserve 1½ cups to use as topping.
Season cheese sauce to taste with salt and pepper.
Pour cheese sauce over pasta in the 9x13 pan. Top with reserved cheese, then with panko bread crumbs.
Bake 12-15 minutes, until golden brown. Let set 5-7 minutes before serving.

Chef's note:
To make roux: combine equal portions of flour and fat. Example: 3 tablespoons flour with 3 tablespoons unsalted butter, and combine over low heat with a whisk. It will have the consistency of wet sand. Cook for 1 minute to cook out the raw flour flavor.

Moroccan Inspired Couscous

While couscous looks like a grain, it is actually small pasta made from semolina flour. The benefits of this type of pasta are that it cooks quickly, and it is great to mix with herbs, spices, and veggies. It also can easily handle additional protein, such as chicken, seafood, meat, or nuts, for a complete meal.

Makes: 8-10 servings

Ingredients
- 2 cups couscous, uncooked
- 1 teaspoon turmeric
- 1 teaspoon paprika
- 1 teaspoon cumin powder
- 1 tablespoon oregano
- 1 teaspoon fresh ginger, grated
- ½ teaspoon kosher salt
- ½ teaspoon fresh ground black pepper
- 4 tablespoons extra-virgin olive oil
- ½ cup parsley, chopped
- ½ cup raisins
- ½ lemon
- 1 plum tomato, chopped

Directions
Cook couscous as per packaged instructions.
Add spices into saucepan, and heat on medium-low until fragrant, about 1 minute.
Add 2 tablespoons olive oil into spices to make paste, heat for an additional minute on low, set aside.
Once couscous is done, remove from heat, add in spice mix, and blend well.
Toss in chopped tomato, parsley, raisins, and remaining olive oil (if desired.)
Squeeze ½ lemon, and mix well.
Serve warm or at room temperature.

Dietary Alternatives
Gluten-free: substitute quinoa for couscous.

Soba Noodle Salad

Soba noodles are made from buckwheat flour. Buckwheat is a gluten-free ancient grain, which has been shown to lower inflammation, and reduce LDL cholesterol levels. Buckwheat also contains a phytonutrient called rutin, which supports the cardiovascular system. Some soba noodles today are made with wheat flour, so be sure to read the label if you are looking for the gluten-free variety.

Makes: 6 servings

Ingredients

- 1 package soba noodles
- 2 bell peppers, julienned
- 2 carrots, julienned
- ½ red onion, julienned
- 1 jalapeno, seeded, minced
- 1 plum tomato, chopped
- 1 yellow squash or zucchini, chopped
- ½ cup micro greens, as garnish (optional)
- 1 tablespoon extra-virgin olive oil

Vinaigrette

- 2 tablespoons peanut butter
- 1 teaspoon ginger root, grated
- 1 lemon, zested, and juiced
- 1 teaspoon raw honey
- 1 tablespoon extra-virgin olive oil
- 1 tablespoon sesame oil
- 1 teaspoon tamari soy sauce

Directions

In a small bowl, combine all of the vinaigrette ingredients with a whisk.
Cook Soba noodles, as per package directions.
Heat olive oil in a sauté pan, add squash, and lightly sauté, about 3 minutes. Add vegetables, along with vinaigrette, toss and serve.

Cherry Pistachio Quinoa Salad

The dark red color of cherries comes from an antioxidant called anthocyanin. According to the American Institute for Cancer Research, during laboratory tests on anthocyanins, they were found to inhibit the growth of cancer cells, and promote self-destruction of the cancer cells. Other studies have also found that the compounds in cherries help reduce arthritis pain, and headaches.

Makes: 4-6 servings

Ingredients
- 1 cup quinoa, cooked
- 4 cups red leaf lettuce, shredded, or mixed field greens
- 1½ cups fresh cherries, pitted, cut in half
- ⅓ cup pistachios, roasted, salted, chopped
- ⅓ cup goat cheese, crumbled
- ¼ cup fresh parsley leaves, rough chop

Vinaigrette
- 2 tablespoons extra-virgin olive oil
- 2 tablespoons unseasoned rice vinegar
- 2 teaspoons raw honey
- ½ teaspoon Dijon mustard
- pinch of kosher salt
- ¼ teaspoon fresh ground black pepper

Directions
Cook quinoa as per package instructions.
In a large bowl, combine quinoa, lettuce, cherries, and parsley.
In a small jar, combine vinaigrette ingredients, and shake to emulsify.
Add vinaigrette to salad, toss to coat, top with goat cheese and pistachios.

4

VEGETABLES

Grilled Green Beans	46
Farro Salad with Peas, Asparagus & Feta	47
Fennel, Carrot & Apple Salad	48
Grilled Orange Sugar Snap Peas	49
Apple & Shaved Brussels Sprouts Salad	50
Spicy Cauliflower	51
Extra Crispy Potatoes	52
Maple Roasted Delicata Squash	53
Roasted Butternut with Grapes	54
Zucchini Pasta	55
Roasted Broccoli & Lemon	56
Lemony Potato Salad	57
Kale & Peach Salad	58
Kale Chips	59

Extra Crispy Potatoes

Kale & Peach Salad

Grilled Orange Sugar Snap Peas

Apple & Shaved Brussels Sprouts Salad

Grilled Green Beans

Forget french fries! These beans are amazing, and so simple. They can easily be thrown on the grill alongside burgers. Green beans are high in lutein and zeaxanthin, which help keep eyes healthy, and vitamin K, which helps maintain bone density and gut health. We recommend enjoying these with lemon pesto (page 100.)

Makes: 4-6 servings, as a side

Ingredients
- 2 pounds green beans
- 2 tablespoons extra-virgin olive oil
- kosher salt
- fresh ground black pepper

Directions
Wash green beans, trim ends.
Place green beans in a large bowl, drizzle in olive oil, season with salt and pepper, and toss to combine.
Grill over medium-high heat, in a vegetable basket, for 5-7 minutes, tossing a couple of times so the beans all start to char.
Depending on the size of your vegetable basket you may need to do in 2-3 batches.
Serve warm, or at room temperature, with lemon pesto (page 100.)

Farro Salad with Peas, Asparagus, & Feta

In spring, our bodies go through a natural cleansing phase, and often we can find ourselves craving bitter foods, such as beer and coffee. This dish is a great way to support our body's cleansing nature. Asparagus, lemon, and radishes all assist in the cleansing process, while oregano and mint help boost our immune system, and keep us cool. This recipe can easily be altered through the seasons by swapping out the asparagus, peas, and radishes for whatever veggies are in season.

Makes: 6 servings, as a side

Ingredients
- 1 cup semi-pearled farro
- ½ pound asparagus, trimmed, cut into ½ inch lengths
- 1 cup peas, fresh or frozen (thawed)
- 4 breakfast radishes, thinly-sliced (if using regular radishes, quarter, then thinly-slice)
- ⅓ cup feta cheese, crumbled
- 2 tablespoons fresh mint, chopped
- 2 tablespoons fresh oregano, chopped

Vinaigrette
- ¼ cup extra-virgin olive oil
- 1 lemon, zested, and 3 tablespoons juice
- 1 tablespoons unseasoned rice vinegar
- 2 teaspoons Dijon mustard
- pinch of kosher salt
- ¼ teaspoon fresh ground black pepper

Directions
Cook farro per package directions, and cool (will be 2 cups after cooking.)
In a large bowl combine farro, asparagus, peas, radishes, and feta.
In a small jar, combine vinaigrette ingredients, and shake to emulsify.
Add vinaigrette to salad, toss to coat, and serve.

Dietary alternatives
Gluten-free: substitute quinoa for farro.
Vegetarian and dairy-free: omit cheese.

Chef's note:
We like the crunch of raw asparagus. If you prefer your asparagus cooked, we recommend grilling it, as a nice option for the salad.

Fennel, Carrot & Apple Salad

Fennel is an excellent digestive aid that helps reduce and calm inflammation. Both carrots and apples also add in some good fiber, which helps regulate blood sugar within the body. This salad is perfect for barbeques and has become a staple for us.

Makes: 6 servings, as a side

Ingredients
- 1 carrot, julienned
- 1 fennel bulb, julienned, core removed.
- 1 apple, julienned

Vinaigrette
- 1 lemon, zested, and 3 tablespoons juice
- 2 tablespoons extra-virgin olive oil
- 2 tablespoons raw honey
- 1½ teaspoons fresh ginger, grated
- ½ teaspoon Dijon mustard
- pinch of kosher salt
- ¼ teaspoon fresh ground black pepper

Directions
In a large bowl, toss apple and fennel in 1 tablespoon of lemon juice. This will prevent oxidation and turning brown. Add in carrots.
In a small jar, combine vinaigrette ingredients, and shake to emulsify.
Pour vinaigrette over apple, fennel and carrot. Toss to coat and serve immediately.

Chef's note:
If you do not get 3 tablespoons of lemon juice from your lemon, you can use rice vinegar, white balsamic, or a second lemon.

Grilled Orange Sugar Snap Peas

This is another great alternative to french fries, or potato salad, when grilling. oranges are a great source of vitamin C. This is high in fiber, and the addition of this great for a healthy digestive system. The sweetness is great for snacking on as

Makes: 4-6, as a side

Ingredients
- 4 cups fresh sugar snap peas
- 1-2 tablespoons extra-virgin olive oil
- 1 orange
- 2 teaspoons toasted black sesame seeds (optional)
- 1 teaspoon fresh ginger, grated
- ½ teaspoon sesame oil
- kosher salt
- fresh ground black pepper

Directions
Preheat grill on medium-high heat.
Remove and discard the stem ends and strings of the sugar snap peas. Place in a large bowl.
Zest orange for 1 tablespoon of zest. Cut orange in half; you will be grilling ½ of the orange.
Toss peas with olive oil, and generously season with salt and pepper.
Place the sugar snap peas onto a grill pan and place the grill pan on the grill. Place the orange half, cut side directly on the grill.
Turn the sugar snap peas several times while grilling, so that they don't get too charred.
Grill for 5-7 minutes or until the pea pods turn a bright green, do not overcook. Once the peas turn a vibrant green color, remove.
Remove orange half when you take peas off the grill.
In a large bowl, toss grilled peas with orange zest, ginger, sesame oil, sesame seeds.
Squeeze the grilled orange half over peas.
Serve warm.

e & Shaved Brussels Sprouts Salad

The fiber in Brussels sprouts has been shown to lower cholesterol, and aid in the prevention of cancer. Being already gluten-free, this salad can easily be altered to support other dietary restrictions.

Makes: 4-6 servings, as a side

Ingredients
- ¼ cup smoked almonds, chopped
- 1 pound Brussels sprouts
- 4 slices bacon, cooked and chopped
- 1 Honeycrisp apple (Fuji, Jazz, or Gala apples work, too)

Vinaigrette
- 2 tablespoons olive oil
- 1 lemon, zested, and 2 tablespoons juice
- 2 tablespoons apple cider
- 2 tablespoons pure maple syrup
- 1 teaspoon Dijon mustard
- pinch of kosher salt
- ¼ teaspoon fresh ground black pepper
- ⅛ cup shaved Parmigiano Reggiano cheese

Directions
Wash the Brussels sprouts, and pat dry.
Cut the Brussels sprouts in half lengthwise through the stem. Using a sharp knife or mandolin, finely slice the Brussels sprouts crosswise to give you fine ribbons.
Remove core, and dice apple. Toss apple in lemon juice to keep from browning. Keep lemon juice for the vinaigrette.
In a small jar, combine all of the vinaigrette ingredients, and shake to emulsify.
To serve, mix the Brussels sprouts and apple together well in a large salad bowl. Lightly dress with the vinaigrette, then top with bacon, almonds, and shaved Parmigiano Reggiano.

Dietary Alternatives
Vegetarian: omit bacon and shaved parmesan.
Nut-free: omit almonds.

Spicy Cauliflower

Cauliflower has been shown to not only fight cancer, but also to lower blood pressure and reduce inflammation. Chili peppers, which makes up sriracha sauce has been shown to improve circulation, reducing pain and inflammation. Scientists at the University of Pittsburgh have also shown that chili peppers may provide cancer fighting benefits by inhibiting the growth of tumors.

Makes: 4-6 servings, as a side

Ingredients
- 1 head cauliflower
- ¼ cup sriracha sauce
- 1 tablespoons olive oil
- 1 clove garlic, minced
- ¼ teaspoon kosher salt
- ¼ teaspoon fresh ground black pepper
- ⅛ cup shaved Parmigiano Reggiano cheese (optional)
- 2 tablespoons parsley, chopped (optional)

Directions
Preheat oven to 425°F.
Chop cauliflower into florets, you may also chop the stem, if desired.
Combine sriracha, olive oil, salt and pepper, with cauliflower, and toss.
Place mixture on baking sheet, roast for approximately 30-35 minutes, or until slightly crispy.
Top with parmesan and parsley, toss and serve.

Extra Crispy Potatoes

These potatoes are a great alternative to tater tots, which can be very high in sodium. Potatoes are a great side for anyone needing a gluten-free alternative. Potatoes are also high in potassium, fiber, and are a great source of energy.

Makes: 4-6 servings, as a side

Ingredients

- 2 pounds waxy or all-purpose potatoes, such as red skin or Yukon Gold.
- 2 tablespoons extra-virgin olive oil
- 1 tablespoon + 1 teaspoon kosher salt
- 2 sprigs rosemary, chopped

Dipping Sauce

- ¼ cup mayonnaise
- 2 teaspoons sriracha sauce

Directions

Preheat oven to 450°F.
Scrub potatoes clean and cut them into 1-inch pieces. Place in a saucepan with a tablespoon of kosher salt, and cover them with about an inch of cold water.
Bring to a boil over high heat, then reduce the heat to a simmer. Cook 4-5 minutes, until the edges are softened, but the centers are still hard.
Drain the water from the pan, using pan lid to keep potatoes from falling out.
Drizzle the potatoes with olive oil, sprinkle with the rosemary, and one teaspoon of kosher salt.
Place lid on the pan and give the potatoes a few good shakes to roughen up the sides and edges.
Spread the potatoes in a single layer on a baking sheet lined with foil or parchment paper.
Bake for 35-40 minutes, flipping potatoes after 20 minutes, until they are evenly browned and crispy.
While potatoes are roasting combine sriracha and mayonnaise in a small bowl.
Serve potatoes immediately, or at room temperature, with sriracha dipping sauce.

Maple Roasted Delicata Squash

Naturally gluten-free, the combination of squash and rosemary helps reduce inflammation and is easy on the digestive system. In a 2003 study published in the *International Journal of Neuroscience* researchers found that rosemary helps in overall memory performance.

Makes: 6-8 servings, as a side

Ingredients
- 3 medium Delicata squash (about 3 pounds,) halved lengthwise, seeded, and cut into ¼-inch thick slices
- 2 fresh rosemary sprigs, chopped
- ½ teaspoon red pepper flakes (optional)
- 2 tablespoons extra-virgin olive oil
- 2 tablespoons pure maple syrup
- kosher salt, to taste
- fresh ground black pepper, to taste

Directions
Preheat the oven to 425°F.
Place the squash, rosemary, and red pepper flakes in a large bowl. Drizzle with olive oil and maple syrup, and sprinkle generously with salt and pepper. Toss to coat.
Spread squash evenly onto two large, rimmed baking sheets. Bake on the upper and lower racks of the oven, tossing, rotating, and switching the pans halfway through cooking, until tender and browned, 25-30 minutes.
Taste and season again with additional salt and pepper, if desired.

Roasted Butternut with Grapes

This quintessential fall dish, highlights the sweetness of the squash and grapes, which is further enhanced by roasting. Grapes and squash are both high in antioxidants that boost our immune system for the colder months. Like most veggies, this dish is also a great source of fiber, and is a perfect gluten-free option.

Makes: 4-6 servings, as a side

Ingredients
- 2 pounds butternut squash, peeled, seeded, cut into 1 ½ -inch pieces
- 1½ cups seedless red grapes (about 8 ounces)
- 1 medium red onion, cut into 1-inch pieces
- 1 sprig rosemary, chopped
- 2 tablespoons extra-virgin olive oil
- 2 tablespoons unsalted butter, melted
- kosher salt
- fresh ground black pepper

Directions
Preheat oven to 425°F.
Combine butternut squash, grapes, onion, and rosemary in large bowl.
Drizzle with olive oil and melted butter.
Season generously with salt and pepper. Toss to coat.
Spread out onto large, rimmed baking sheet covered in foil or parchment paper.
Roast until squash and onion begin to brown, stirring occasionally, about 50 minutes.
Transfer to platter, and serve.

Zucchini Pasta

Many times we find that what people enjoy about pasta is the sauce, or whatever goes on the pasta, rather than the pasta itself. This is an amazing alternative for anyone looking to increase their overall vegetable intake, or has dietary issues with milk, eggs, or gluten. We recommend this pasta becoming a staple in your diet. To even further increase your vegetable intake, serve with Romesco sauce (page 103.)

Makes: 4 servings, as a side

Ingredients
- 2 medium zucchinis
- 1 tablespoons extra-virgin olive oil
- kosher salt, to taste
- fresh ground black pepper, to taste

Directions
Cut zucchini into thin, noodle-like strips (a mandolin works well, or see Chef's note below.)
Once your zucchini is sliced, heat a sauté pan or wok on medium-high, and add olive oil. Sauté zucchini for 3 minutes, or until al dente.
Remove zucchini with slotted spoon. Season with salt and pepper, or top with Romesco sauce, and serve.

Chef's note:
If a mandolin is not available, you can use a spiralizer, or julienne peeler.
If using a julienne peeler, decrease cooking time to 2 minutes.
To reduce the amount of water when cooking, use smaller zucchinis that have less seeds. When slicing zucchini, or using a peeler, discard the slices that are mostly seeds.

Roasted Broccoli & Lemon

Broccoli is one of the healthiest veggies available, due to its anti-cancer properties. It also has a high amount of vitamin C and K, which help protect our bones and keep them strong. Additionally, a study published in March of 2009 from the journal *Clinical Immunology*, found the compound called sulforaphane in broccoli protects us from respiratory conditions by reducing inflammation.

Makes: 4 servings, as a side

Ingredients
- 1 pound broccoli florets
- 2 tablespoons olive oil
- kosher salt, to taste
- fresh ground black pepper, to taste
- 1 lemon, cut in half

Directions
Preheat oven to 500°F, or broil.
In a large bowl, toss the broccoli with the oil. Salt and pepper to taste. Arrange the broccoli and lemon in a single layer on a baking sheet and roast, turning broccoli once, for 12 minutes, or until just tender.
Place the broccoli in a serving bowl. Squeeze roasted lemon over the top using tongs, so you do not burn yourself.

Lemony Potato Salad

We can just about guarantee this will become one of your favorite potato salads. Potato salad historically is very heavy, but the addition of lemon really lightens the salad, while still providing that comforting taste of traditional potato salad.

Makes: 6 servings, as a side

Ingredients
- 2 pounds baby red skin potatoes, cut into quarters
- 1 cup celery, diced small
- ½ cup green onions, thinly sliced (about 3)
- ¼ cup mayonnaise
- 1 lemon, zested, and 2 tablespoons juice
- 2 teaspoons whole-grain mustard
- 1 teaspoons Dijon mustard
- ¾ teaspoon salt
- ¼ teaspoon fresh ground black pepper

Directions
In a large Dutch oven, cover quartered potatoes with cold water.
Bring to a boil, cook 5-6 minutes, or just until tender.
Drain, and let cool 5 minutes.
Whisk together remaining ingredients in a large bowl.
Add cooled potatoes, toss to coat. Chill, and serve cold.

Kale & Peach Salad

Prior to Paige creating this recipe, I, despite being an integrative nutrition coach, was not a big kale salad fan. However, this recipe changed my mind. Kale is a nutritional powerhouse, loaded with nutrients, protein, and fiber. Peaches are high in vitamin A and C, which help improve both skin and eyes.

Makes: 2 servings, as an entree, 4, as a side

Ingredients
- 1 small bunch kale, julienned (4-5 cups)(Red Russian kale or Tuscan/ Dinosaur kale)
- 2 peaches, diced
- ¼ cup slivered almonds, toasted
- ¼ cup Parmigiano Reggiano cheese, shaved

Vinaigrette
- 2 tablespoons rice vinegar
- 2 tablespoons extra-virgin olive oil
- 1 tablespoon raw honey
- 1 teaspoon Dijon mustard
- ½ teaspoon ginger, grated
- pinch of kosher salt
- ¼ teaspoon fresh ground black pepper

Directions
In a large bowl, mix kale, peaches, and almonds.
In a small jar, combine all vinaigrette ingredients, and shake to emulsify.
Pour ¾ of the vinaigrette on the salad, and toss to combine. Depending on how much kale you used, you may want to add the remaining vinaigrette.
Top with Parmigiano Reggiano cheese.
Serve immediately.

Chef's note:
Kale used should be fresh. Older kale that has been sitting around gets tough, and loses its taste. We recommend using kale fresh from a garden or farmer's market, if possible.

Kale Chips

Several studies have found kale to be beneficial in the prevention of cancer. In 2005 a study published in the *International Urology and Nephrology Journal* found kale to have the highest protective benefits against bladder cancer among all other foods tested.

Makes: 4 servings, as a side

Ingredients
- 1 small bunch kale
- 1 tablespoon extra-virgin olive oil
- ¼ teaspoon Himalayan salt, to taste
- ¼ teaspoon fresh ground black pepper, to taste

Directions
Preheat oven to 325°F.
Fold kale in half lengthwise and remove leaves from stem.
Discard stem and tear leaves into chip size pieces.
Coat with olive oil, salt and pepper.
Lay leaves flat on baking sheet so that they are not touching each other.
Bake for 8-10 minutes until edges are slightly brown, and leaves are crisp.
Remove and serve.

Chef's note:
Watch chips carefully, cooking time may vary. Try these flavor alternatives:
Spicy: added 1 teaspoon sriracha sauce with olive oil, increase according to preferred taste
Sweet: add 1½ teaspoon honey to olive oil
Salt & Vinegar: add 1 teaspoon vinegar to olive oil and finish with salt.

5

SOUP

Bone Broth	62
Sausage & Lentil Soup	63
Chicken Noodle Soup	64
Oxtail Stew	65
Tomato Basil Soup	66
Creamy Potato Soup	67

Top: Roasted Tomato Basil Soup
Bottom: Gazpacho

Bone Broth

It should probably be renamed "elixir of life." Bone broth is loaded with vitamins and minerals, which boost the immune system, and are easily absorbed in our bodies. It also contains glucosamine, and chondroitin, which are great for joint and bone health, as well as, gelatin, which assists in the prevention of degenerative joint disease. The uses for this broth are endless. Make a clear soup, mixed with sautéed veggies, rice, or udon for a heartier soup, or enjoy it like tea.

Makes: 6 servings

Ingredients
- 2 pounds bones (beef, chicken, pork…etc.)
- 6-8 carrots, roughly chopped
- 6 stalks celery, roughly chopped
- 2 white or yellow onions, halved
- 8 gloves garlic, smashed
- bundle of herbs: use a mix of your favorite (parsley, rosemary, thyme, oregano)
- 1 teaspoon Himalayan salt
- 1 teaspoon apple cider vinegar
- Water

Directions
Place everything in a large slow-cooker and cover bones with water. Cook on low for 12 hours. Allow to cool. Remove bones and vegetables with a slotted spoon.
Once all the large contents are removed strain the broth through a fine mesh strainer or cheesecloth.
Serve, or freeze for future use.

Chef's note:
We recommend using bones from local farms, or butchers, if possible, to ensure quality.
Adding this to other dishes will increase the nutritional density and flavor of those dishes.
If roasting a chicken, you can put the chicken bones in a slow-cooker and make bone broth.
If you make a recipe that only uses parsley leaves, freeze the parsley stems, then use them to add more flavor to your next broth recipe.

Sausage & Lentil Soup

There is something very comforting about this soup. The store bought, canned variety, is very high in sodium, and lacks fresh ingredients. We recommend getting a good sausage from your farmer's market, and using bone broth to increase both the flavor, and nutritional density of this soup.

Makes: 6 servings

Ingredients
- 1 pound hot Italian sausage, removed from casing.
- 1 cup onion, chopped
- 1 cup carrot, chopped
- 1 cup celery, chopped
- 1 cup fennel stalks, chopped (optional)
- 2 large garlic cloves, minced
- 2 cups french green lentils
- 4-5 cup bone broth, or chicken stock
- kosher salt, to taste
- fresh ground black pepper, to taste

Directions
In a large pot, brown sausage over medium heat, about 5-7 minutes, break up with a spatula while cooking. Add vegetables and garlic. Season with a pinch of salt and pepper, cook for 2 minutes.
Add lentils and 4 cups bone broth or chicken stock, and bring to a boil. Reduce heat to medium-low, and simmer until lentils are tender, about 30 minutes.
Season to taste with salt and pepper. Thin soup with broth or stock to desired consistency.

Chef's note:
When using a fennel bulb in other recipes, go ahead and chop off the fennel stalks, and freeze for future use. Use the stalks later to add more flavor to a soup, or vegetable stock.

Chicken Noodle Soup

Our mothers and grandmothers had it right, when we weren't feeling well, we got chicken soup. What could be better than a nutritionally dense soup with homemade chicken broth, veggies, and small noodles or rice? While this soup is packed with nutrients, it's also very easy on the digestive system, allowing our body the energy needed to heal itself. Not only is it great for when we aren't feeling well, but it's a great soup every time we just need some good comfort food.

Makes: 6-8 servings

Ingredients
- 7 cups chicken bone broth
- 2½ cups chopped roasted chicken
- ¾ cup white or yellow onion, diced
- 1 cup celery, diced
- 1 cup carrots, diced
- 1 clove garlic, grated
- 1 recipe for homemade egg noodles (page 37)
- kosher salt, to taste
- fresh ground black pepper, to taste
- 2 tablespoons finely chopped fresh parsley leaves

Directions
Bring broth to boil for 2 minutes in a large stockpot, over high heat. Add onion, carrots, celery, and garlic. Cook for 3-4 additional minutes.
Add noodles, and cook 5-6 minutes until noodles are done, and vegetables are tender.
Remove from heat, add chicken and parsley. Season with salt and pepper, to taste.

Oxtail Stew

It wasn't until a farmer introduced me to oxtail, that I became a fan. It's amazingly tender and nutrient dense, as well as, high in gelatin. Oxtail is usually cheaper than other cuts of meat, which makes this stew more affordable. We recommend getting the tails from the farmer's market, if possible. If tails are unavailable, other bones, such as shin bones, can be used.

Makes: 6-8 servings

Ingredients
- 2 oxtails, jointed and cut into pieces
- 1 tablespoon unsalted butter
- 1 cup white or yellow onion, chopped
- 1½ cup celery, chopped
- 1½ cup carrots, chopped
- 1 cup leeks, chopped (white and light green only)
- 5 cloves garlic, crushed
- 1 teaspoon kosher salt
- 1 teaspoon fresh ground black pepper
- 1 teaspoon dried oregano
- 1 teaspoon dried rosemary
- 1 teaspoons dried thyme
- 2 bay leaves
- ½ teaspoon dried basil
- 4 leaves kale
- potato starch
- water

Directions
Preheat oven to 350°F.
Place oxtail on cookie sheet, sprinkle with pinch of salt and pepper, and roast for 30 minutes.
Place butter in a large Dutch oven, add in onions, celery, carrots, leeks, and garlic. Sauté until onions are translucent, 5-7 minutes.
Add in herbs and oxtail.
Fill pot with water to cover everything.
Bring to a boil and reduce to low heat, simmer for 4 hours.
Add kale until wilted,
To thicken, add in potato starch mixed with cold water until reaching desired consistency.
Serve hot.

Chef's note:
Leeks can be omitted. Increase onion to 1½ cups.
If oxtails are not available, shin bones, or short ribs, make a great stew as well.
Tails are fatty, which lends the stew it's amazing flavor. If you would like to remove the fat, then prior to thickening, pour the liquid only through a fat separator. Pour off the fat, and add the remaining liquid back into the vegetable mixture.

Tomato Basil Soup

Research published in *Journal of Agriculture and Food Chemistry* found that for the lycopene in tomatoes to be utilized by the body, the tomatoes had to be simmered in fat. This soup accomplishes that, has amazing flavor, and can also be utilized as a tomato sauce before thinning with broth.

Makes: 6-8 servings

Ingredients
- ¼ cup extra-virgin olive oil
- 1½ cups carrots, peeled and diced
- 2 cups white onion, diced
- 2 teaspoons dried basil
- 2 -28 ounce cans whole, peeled, tomatoes
- 2 cups vegetable broth
- ½ teaspoon kosher salt
- ¼ teaspoon fresh ground black pepper
- 2 cups additional vegetable broth (optional)

Directions
Preheat oven to 375°F.
In a large oven proof pan, heat the olive oil over medium-high heat until simmering. Add carrots and onion, cook until they begin to soften, about 10 minutes. Add basil, and 2 cups vegetable broth. Cook until vegetables are completely soft, about 5 additional minutes.
Add salt, pepper, and tomatoes, crushing the tomatoes with a spatula or wooden spoon. Cover the pan with a tight fitting lid and place in the oven for 1½ hours.
After allowing soup to cool for 10 minutes, purée with an immersion blender, or food processor until smooth (or your desired consistency.) Do so in batches if using a food processor or stand blender.
If desired, stir in additional vegetable broth, little by little over low heat, until desired texture is reached. Season to taste with salt and pepper. Serve warm.

Chef's note:
Roasting the soup in the oven intensifies the tomato flavor, and thickens the soup.

For a really creamy tomato soup, use heavy cream instead of vegetable broth to thin to desired texture.

Canned tomatoes are used for this recipe because most people look to make tomato soup during the winter months, when fresh tomatoes are not at their peak. Use 3½ pounds of fresh tomatoes if you are able to get good, fresh tomatoes.

To serve cold as a gazpacho, thin to desired consistency with vegetable broth, adding diced cucumbers, zucchini, corn, peppers and fresh tomatoes to top. Drizzle with extra-virgin olive oil and fresh julienned basil.

Creamy Potato Soup

Sometimes a bowl of soup just comes down to food that feeds our soul and makes us feel at home again. Making this tasty potato soup, we are able to control the quality of ingredients, and the sodium content, which makes it a healthier alternative to soup from a can.

Makes: 6-8 servings

Ingredients
- 6 strips of bacon, cut in ½ inch pieces
- 4 cups whole milk
- 1 cup celery, diced
- 1 cup carrots, diced
- 1 cup white or yellow onion, diced
- 6 cups of potatoes, peeled, diced (Yukon gold or russet)
- 3 tablespoons all-purpose flour
- 3 tablespoons bacon grease
- 2 teaspoons kosher salt
- fresh ground black pepper, to taste
- 4-5 green onions, sliced for garnish
- cheddar cheese, shredded, for garnish

Directions
In a large stock pot, cook bacon until crisp. Remove the bacon, place on a paper towel lined plate, and reserve 3 tablespoons of bacon grease. Remaining bacon grease can be saved for future use.
Place potatoes in a separate pot just covered with cold water. Bring to a boil and cook for 7-10 minutes, until potatoes are tender.
Add celery, carrots, and onions to the stock pot in which you cooked the bacon, and sauté for 5 minutes, stirring occasionally. Sprinkle flour over carrots, onions, and celery, and stir until combined. Cook for an additional minute, stirring occasionally.
While stirring, add milk to stock pot. Continue cooking until the milk reaches a simmer.
Add potatoes, and their water (approximately 3 cups,) to stock pot.
Season with salt and pepper.
Reduce heat to low, cover pan and simmer for 10-15 minutes until the potatoes, carrots, onions and, celery are soft, stirring occasionally.
Taste, and adjust salt and pepper, as desired.
Serve warm, topped with bacon, cheese, and green onions.

Chef's Note:
Boiling the potatoes in a separate pan will reduce the overall cook time, as you do not want to boil the milk. The potato water is starchy and will also help thicken the soup.

6

POULTRY

Braised Chicken Thighs with Fennel & Blood Oranges	70
5 Spice & Ginger Grilled Chicken Breast	71
Honey Lime Grilled Chicken Breast	72
Herb Roasted Duck	73
Bourbon Maple Syrup Chicken Legs	74
Chicken Tenders	75

Braised Chicken Thighs with Fennel & Blood Oranges

Braised Chicken Thighs with Fennel & Blood Oranges

The University of Perugia, in Italy, found that pasture raised chicken had a higher level of antioxidants, and lower risk of oxidated stress, than conventionally raised chickens. We recommend visiting your local farms, and giving pasture raised chicken a try. We know that oranges are great sources of vitamin C. Did you know, however, that you can eat the rind of the oranges? Actually, many of the health benefits of an orange are located in the rind.

Makes: 2-4 servings

Ingredients
- 4 bone in, skin on, chicken thighs
- 2 tablespoons extra-virgin olive oil
- 1 large fennel bulb, sliced
- 2 blood oranges, thinly sliced, seeds discarded
- 1 tablespoon fresh thyme, plus some additional for garnish
- 2 tablespoons pure maple syrup
- ⅓ cup dry white wine or chicken stock
- kosher salt, to taste
- fresh ground black pepper, to taste

Directions
Remove chicken thighs from refrigerator 20 minutes prior to cooking.
Preheat oven to 425°F.
Season the chicken on both sides with salt and pepper.
Using a large ovenproof pan, or a Dutch oven, large enough to hold all chicken thighs in a single layer, heat the olive oil over medium heat.
Once the oil is hot, add the chicken, skin side down.
Sear the chicken approximately 5-6 minutes per side, until golden brown.
Remove the chicken from the pan, and set aside.
With the pan still hot, add the fennel and thyme, season with salt and pepper, and stir frequently.
After 2-3 minutes, add the blood oranges, continue cooking until the fennel has softened, and the brown bits on the bottom of the pan have loosened, about 6-8 minutes total.
Add the white wine.
Nestle the chicken thighs, skin side up, in the fennel mixture.
Pour the maple syrup over the chicken, transfer the pan to the oven, and bake for 15-20 minutes.
Scatter fresh thyme leaves over the top, and serve.

Five-Spice & Ginger Grilled Chicken Breast

The main spices in Chinese five-spice are anise, clove, cinnamon, fennel seeds, and pepper. In Chinese medicine, five-spice is believed to aid the digestive and circulatory system, so this makes a great recipe to use to calm the digestive system, or when needing an added boost for immune health. Using honey for medicinal purposes has been found as far back as ancient Egypt, and is commonly used today to ease sore throats. The *Archives of Pediatrics and Adolescent Medicine* published a study that showed an increase in sleep, and decrease in coughing among children who had used honey to combat a cough, versus those who took cough syrup, or nothing at all.

Makes: 4 servings

Ingredients
- 4 (6-ounce) boneless, skinless, chicken breasts
- 1 tablespoon Chinese five-spice powder
- 1 teaspoon fresh ginger, grated, tightly packed
- 1 tablespoon extra-virgin olive oil
- 2 tablespoons raw honey
- ¼ teaspoon kosher salt
- ¼ teaspoon fresh ground

Directions
Place chicken breasts in gallon size zip-top bag. Using a mallet, pound each to an even thickness of ½ inch. Do not make them any thinner, or they could dry out.

Add all ingredients to the bag of chicken, and shake to coat. Refrigerate chicken for 1-2 hours. Remove chicken from fridge while you heat the grill.

Light the grill, building a hot fire, or heat your gas grill to high. Once grill is fully heated, place chicken on the grill.

Discard remaining marinade that was in the bag with the chicken.

Cook until undersides are browned and chicken is about halfway cooked, about 3-4 minutes. Flip breasts and grill until cooked through, 3-4 minutes more.

Transfer chicken to a platter. Serve hot, or at room temperature.

Honey Lime Grilled Chicken Breast

During the summer months, our ovens barely ever turn on. Grilling for us is a great way to change the taste of food from the typical roasting, braising, or baking we are used to during the cooler months. Chicken breasts are a great form of lean protein, the addition of the lime helps brighten the dish, and the honey will add a hint of sweetness. This is the perfect way to prepare chicken for a salad, or even chicken tacos.

Makes: 4 servings

Ingredients
- 4 (6-ounce) chicken breasts, boneless, skinless
- 1 lime, zested, and ¼ cup of juice
- ¼ cup extra-virgin olive oil
- 2 tablespoons raw honey
- 1 tablespoon Dijon mustard
- ½ teaspoon kosher salt
- ½ teaspoon black pepper

Directions
Place chicken breasts in gallon size zip-top bag. Using a mallet, pound each to an even thickness of ½-inch. Do not make them any thinner, or they will dry out.

In a small jar, combine lime juice, zest, oil, honey, mustard, salt and pepper, to create a marinade. Shake well to combine. Pour ½ cup of marinade (keeping 2-3 tablespoons in jar) on chicken in bag. Refrigerate marinated chicken for 1-2 hours.

Remove chicken from fridge while you heat the grill.

Light the grill, building a hot fire, or heat your gas grill to high. Once grill is fully heated, place chicken on the grill.

Discard remaining marinade that was in the bag with the chicken.

Cook until undersides are browned and chicken is about halfway cooked, 3-4 minutes. Flip breasts and grill until cooked through, 3-4 additional minutes.

Transfer chicken to a platter. Drizzle the 2-3 tablespoons of reserved marinade from the jar on the chicken.

Herb Roasted Duck

Duck fat has been found to be healthier than other animal fats, due to it being lower in saturated fat content. Many restaurants are beginning to use duck fat when making french fries, and other dishes. Duck is also a great alternative to roasted chicken, having its own great, unique flavor.

Makes: 4 servings

Ingredients
- 1 whole duck, 5-6 lbs.
- 2 tablespoons fresh parsley, chopped
- 1 tablespoon fresh basil, chopped
- 1 tablespoon fresh oregano, chopped
- 1 teaspoon kosher salt
- ¼ teaspoon fresh ground black pepper

Directions
Bring duck to room temperature 20 minutes prior to roasting.
Preheat oven to 425°F.
Remove excess skin from duck neck and hind. (Skin can be saved, and fat rendered, for other uses.)
Truss the duck and prick the skin heavily (this is needed to release the excess fat from the skin while roasting.) Dry thoroughly.
Combine herbs with salt and pepper, and massage onto duck.
Place duck in roasting pan, and roast for 30 minutes.
Reduce heat to 350°F, and cook for an additional hour.
Occasionally remove accumulated fat from pan with a bulb baster.

Chef's note:
Save the accumulated duck fat, and store in the fridge for later use.

Bourbon Maple Syrup Chicken Legs

The first time I had the sauce in this recipe was at my brother's. I admit it, I took way more "taste tests" than were required. Bourbon and maple syrup...we think that just about explains it. This is simply good food.

Makes: 4 servings

Ingredients
- 3-4 pounds chicken legs
- kosher salt, to taste
- fresh ground black pepper, to taste
- ½ cup pure maple syrup
- ½ cup Bourbon

Directions
Preheat oven to 400°F.
Place legs in a large baking dish and season with salt and pepper on all sides.
Bake for 45 minutes, flip the legs, and bake for an additional 10 minutes.
Meanwhile combine bourbon and maple syrup in an uncovered pot. Allow to simmer, stirring occasionally, for 30 minutes, or until reduced by half. The end result should resemble a syrup.
Remove chicken from oven, drizzle with the bourbon maple syrup, and serve.

Chicken Tenders

Do you remember the moist mayonnaise chicken your mom or grandma used to make? This recipe takes it to the next level, omitting the mayonnaise, but retaining the moisture by using yogurt. These also are great dipped in lemon pesto (page 100,) or romesco sauce (page 103.) This is a great way to get some good, quality, lean protein, and works great for kids.

Makes: 4 servings

Ingredients
- 3-4 chicken breasts, boneless, skinless
- 1 cup plain yogurt
- ½ teaspoon smoked paprika
- ½ teaspoon kosher salt
- ½ teaspoon garlic powder

Coating
- 2 cups panko bread crumbs
- 1 teaspoon smoked paprika
- 1 teaspoon kosher salt
- 1 teaspoon garlic powder

Directions
In a large bowl, mix yogurt and spices together.
Cut chicken into 3-4 approximately 1-inch strips per breast, depending on the size of the chicken breast.
Place chicken in yogurt, and stir to coat. Allow to marinate for a minimum of 30 minutes, can be done up to a day ahead.
Preheat oven to 450°F. Place baking stone or baking sheet in oven while it is preheating. This will help the bottom of the chicken tenders to crisp.
Mix panko bread crumbs with coating spices in a shallow pan. Remove chicken tenders from yogurt mix and place in panko spice mix , coat chicken on all sides. Place chicken tenders on a plate.
Once all chicken is coated in panko, remove hot baking stone from oven, place chicken tenders on the hot baking stone. Place the stone back in the oven, and cook chicken for 18 minutes.
Serve with your favorite dipping sauce.

Dietary Alternative:
Gluten-free: Replace Panko for gluten-free bread crumbs, or use toasted quinoa.
Dairy-free: Coconut yogurt can be used in place of plain yogurt

Chef's note:
When removing chicken tenders from the yogurt, remove excess yogurt. You do want some yogurt to still cover your chicken, as this will keep it moist while cooking, but if there is too much yogurt, the panko will not get crispy.

7

MEAT

Prosciutto & Rosemary Wrapped Pork Tenderloin	78
Slow-cooker Carnitas	79
Pork Shoulder & Ginger Beer	80
Braised Short Ribs	81
Hearty Beef Stew	82
Grilled Tri-Tip	83

Slow-cooker Carnitas

Prosciutto & Rosemary Wrapped Pork Tenderloin

This is one of our favorites to make when entertaining friends and family. Pork tenderloin is considered a lean protein option, as there is less fat compared to a pork chop. Pork tenderloin is also a good source of selenium, which helps aid metabolism.

Makes: 6-8 servings

Ingredients
- 12 thin slices prosciutto (about ¼ pound)
- 2 (1-1½ pound) pork tenderloins
- 1 tablespoon fresh rosemary, chopped
- ½ teaspoon kosher salt
- ½ teaspoon fresh ground black pepper
- 1 tablespoon extra-virgin olive oil

Directions
Put oven rack in middle position, and preheat oven to 425°F.
Place 6 prosciutto slices on work surface lengthwise, slightly overlapping, with short ends near you.
Pat 1 pork tenderloin dry and sprinkle all over with ¼ teaspoon salt, ¼ teaspoon pepper, and ½ tablespoon of rosemary.
Place tenderloin in middle of prosciutto (tucking end of tenderloin underneath if very thin), then wrap prosciutto around pork to enclose.
Place remaining 6 slices of prosciutto on work surface, as before, then wrap second tenderloin in same manner.
Transfer tenderloins, seam sides down and 2 inches apart, to a small roasting pan. Brush prosciutto all over with olive oil.
Roast until thermometer, inserted in center of meat, registers 150°F, about 25 minutes.
Transfer to a cutting board and let stand 10 minutes before slicing.

Slow-cooker Carnitas

Slow-cookers are a must for anyone with a busy schedule. Toss ingredients in when you leave, and have dinner ready when you get home. This makes a large amount, so it's also perfect for freezing, and then using later for a quick dinner.

Makes: 8-10 servings

Ingredients
- 6-7 pounds boneless country-style pork ribs, or pork shoulder (Boston butt,) cut into 1½ -inch pieces
- 2½ tablespoons kosher salt
- 2 teaspoons fresh ground black pepper
- 2 tablespoons dried oregano (preferably Mexican)
- 2 large white or yellow onions, cut into 8 pieces per onion

Directions
Place pork in bowl of slow-cooker. Toss with salt, black pepper, and dried oregano, to coat.
Place onion pieces atop pork.
Cover slow-cooker, and cook pork until meat is very tender and falling apart, about 6 hours on low, or 3½ hours on high.
Using slotted spoon, transfer pork to cutting board.
Reserve onion pieces.
Using 2 forks, shred pork, and transfer carnitas to platter.

Serve with:
- guacamole
- queso fresco
- reserved onion pieces
- red peppers, diced
- shredded romaine lettuce
- corn and/or flour tortillas
- Salsa

Pork Shoulder with Ginger Beer

Ginger has a long history in Indian and Asian culture. Chinese medicine uses ginger for stomach related issues, treating arthritis, and heart conditions. At the University of Maryland, a study found that those suffering from osteoarthritis experienced less pain when taking ginger extract.

Makes: 8 servings

Ingredients
- 1 skinless, bone-in pork shoulder (Boston butt, 5-6 pounds)
- 2 tablespoons kosher salt
- 2 teaspoons fresh ground black pepper
- 1 cup apple cider
- 1 bottle ginger beer
- 3 sprigs of rosemary
- 4 shallots, peeled, cut in half

Directions
Preheat oven to 325°F.
Season pork with salt and pepper.
Place shallots in an oven-safe Dutch oven.
Place pork, fat side up, on top of shallots in the Dutch oven.
Add remaining ingredients.
Cover and roast until pork is well browned, and very tender, approximately 3½-4 hours, depending on size of pork shoulder. Pork should easily pull away from the bone.
Let pork rest at least 10 minutes before serving.

Braised Short Ribs

When the weather starts to cool, this is one of the first hearty recipes that gets made every year. These short ribs are braised in a combination of red wine, and beef broth. Red wine contains a compound called resveratrol, which helps plants survive and repair themselves after stress, or illness. A study from Harvard Medical School found anti-aging benefits among resveratrol that can help extend quality of life.

Makes: 6-8 servings

Ingredients
- 6 pounds bone-in short ribs
- 1½ cups onions, chopped
- 1½ cups celery, chopped
- 1½ cups carrots, peeled, chopped
- 3 garlic cloves, rough chop
- 2 cups dry red wine
- 3 cups low-salt beef broth
- 2 tablespoons tomato paste
- 1 tablespoon instant coffee or espresso
- ½ cup large raisins, mixed
- 2 tablespoons fresh parsley, chopped
- 3 fresh thyme sprigs
- 2 fresh rosemary sprigs
- kosher salt
- fresh ground black pepper

Directions

Preheat oven to 350°F
Liberally sprinkle ribs with salt and pepper.
Add ribs to enameled cast iron pan, or heavy oven-proof pot.
Add remaining ingredients with beef broth and red wine to just cover ribs.
Cover, cook in oven for 2 hours. Turn ribs, and add more liquid to just cover, if necessary.
Cook, covered, for an addition 30-60 minutes, until tender.
Transfer ribs to a plate. With a spoon, remove fat from the surface of the sauce.
Puree sauce with immersion blender.
Place pot on stove, at medium heat.
Season sauce to taste with salt and pepper.
Return ribs to pot. Simmer to warm.
Serve over mashed potatoes.

Hearty Beef Stew

During the winter months, our bodies digest food more slowly. We find ourselves requiring warmer foods, such as root veggies, and slow-cooked meats. Stew is the quintessential winter meal, having the starchiness of the potatoes, and the hearty slow-cooked beef.

Makes: 4-6 servings

Ingredients
- 6 medium potatoes, medium-diced
- 2 pounds beef, cubed
- 2 medium white or yellow onions, medium-diced
- 8 carrots, medium-diced
- 4 celery ribs, medium-diced
- 2 bay leaves
- ¼ cup tapioca
- 1½ teaspoons dried thyme
- 1 tablespoon coconut oil, or ghee
- 3 cups tomato puree
- ½ teaspoon Himalayan salt
- ¼ teaspoon fresh ground black pepper

Directions
Add all ingredients to the crockpot.
Cook on low for 6 hours.
Serve hot.

Grilled Tri-Tip

Tri-tip is cut from the bottom of the sirloin, in a small triangular shape. It tends to look similar to flank steak, and it is also referred to as Santa Maria steak. A good source of vitamin D, B12, and Iron, tri-tip cuts are gaining in popularity, as they are also leaner cut of beef.

Makes: 4-6 servings

Ingredients
- 1 tri-tip steak, 2-3 pounds
- kosher salt
- fresh ground black pepper

Marinade
- ¼ cup extra-virgin olive oil
- 4 medium garlic cloves, finely chopped
- 2 tablespoons fresh rosemary, chopped
- 2 tablespoons fresh oregano, chopped
- 1 medium lemon, zested and juiced

Directions
Combine marinade ingredients in zip-top bag. Marinate tri-tip at least 1 hour, up to 24 hours.

Bring tri-tip to room temperature 30 minutes prior to grilling. Remove from marinade and liberally season all sides with salt and pepper. Discard marinade.

Preheat grill. Place the tri-tip on the grill, close the cover, and grill over high heat for 5 minutes. Rotate the tri-tip 90 degrees, close the cover, and grill until the underside is deep brown and grill marks have appeared, approximately an additional 5-6 minutes.

Flip the tri-tip and continue grilling, rotating 90 degrees after 5 minutes. Grill an additional 5-6 minutes, until the tri-tip has reached an internal temperature of 125°F (for medium rare,) on an instant-read thermometer, about 20-22 minutes total.

Transfer the meat to a cutting board, tent loosely with foil, and let rest for 10-15 minutes. Slice against the grain and serve with chimichurri sauce (page 102.)

8

SEAFOOD

Salmon with Caramelized Onions & Apples	86
Seared Scallops	87
Cod en Papillote with Tomatoes & Asparagus	88
Bacon-wrapped Jalapeno & Cheese Stuffed Shrimp	89

Salmon with Caramelized Onions & Apples

Salmon with Caramelized Onions & Apples

An excellent source of Omega-3's, salmon is great for helping reduce inflammation, and is often recommended as part of a heart healthy diet. Salmon actually contains particular peptides that have been shown to be effective in supporting joints, controlling insulin, as well as, inflammation within the digestive system.

Makes: 4 servings

Ingredients

- 4 wild king salmon filets, skin on (5-6 ounces each)
- 2 white or yellow onions, peeled, halved, and thinly-sliced
- 2 medium apples, diced (Honeycrisp, Jazz, Fuji)
- 1 tablespoon rosemary, chopped
- 1 lemon, zested, and juice from half of the lemon
- 2 tablespoons unsalted butter
- 2 tablespoons extra-virgin olive oil
- kosher salt
- fresh ground black pepper

Directions

In a large sauté pan, add 1 tablespoon butter, 1 tablespoon olive oil, and the onions. Cover and cook over medium heat, stirring occasionally, for 15-20 minutes, or until onions are soft and a deep golden brown. Season with salt and pepper. Remove from pan, and set aside.

While onions are cooking, dice apples. In a bowl, add the juice of half of the lemon to the diced apples, toss to coat, and set aside.

Bring the salmon to room temperature 10 minutes before cooking. Season both sides of the salmon with salt and pepper.

Increase the heat to medium-high, and heat remaining butter and oil in the pan the onions were just cooked in. Place the salmon, skin side up, in the pan. Cook until golden brown on one side, approximately 3-4 minutes. Turn salmon over with a spatula, add diced apples, rosemary, and return the caramelized onions to the pan. Cook until the salmon feels firm to the touch, about 3 more minutes.

Divide the onions and apples among plates, and serve salmon on top. Garnish with the lemon zest and rosemary.

Seared Scallops

High in vitamins and minerals, such as B12, iodine, selenium, zinc, and magnesium, scallops help boost the immune system. They also provide support for the thyroid and metabolism, and are a great form of lean protein.

Makes: 4 servings

Ingredients
- 1 to 1¼ pounds dry sea scallops, approximately 16
- 1 tablespoon unsalted butter
- 1 tablespoon extra-virgin olive oil
- kosher salt
- fresh ground black pepper

Directions
Remove the small-side muscle from the scallops, rinse with cold water, and thoroughly pat dry.
Add the butter and oil to a 12 or 14-inch sauté pan, on high heat.
Season the scallops with salt and pepper. Once the fat begins to smoke, gently add the scallops, making sure they do not touch each other.
Sear the scallops for 1½ minutes on each side. The scallops should have a ¼-inch golden crust on each side, while still being translucent in the center.
Serve immediately with romesco sauce (page 103,) or chimichurri sauce (page 102.)

Cod en Papillote with Tomatoes & Asparagus

Cod is a good form of lean protein. It is also a good source of iodine, which supports the thyroid, as well as, B12 and magnesium, for metabolic support. Cooking fish en papillote (in parchment envelope) allows the nutrients that are normally lost in water to be absorbed through the veggies.

Makes: 4 servings

Ingredients
- Parchment paper
- 4 cod fillets (6 ounces each)
- 1 pound asparagus, washed, woody ends trimmed
- 2 tablespoons + 2 teaspoons extra-virgin olive oil
- 1 cup grape tomatoes, halved
- 1 teaspoon kosher salt
- ½ teaspoon fresh ground black pepper
- ¼ cup dry white wine
- 16-20 fresh basil leaves

Directions
Preheat oven to 425°F.
Fold four 15-inch-square pieces of parchment in half. Starting at the fold of each piece, draw half a large heart shape. Cut along lines, and open.
Season both sides of cod filet with salt and pepper.
Place 5 asparagus stalks inside next to the crease on each piece of parchment, place cod on top of asparagus.
Top cod with 4-5 basil leaves per filet, add 10-12 tomato halves per filet.
Top each filet with 2 teaspoons olive oil, and 1 tablespoon wine.
Fold other half of parchment over fish. Starting at top of each parchment half-heart, make small, tight, overlapping folds along outside edge to seal packet; twist tail ends tightly to seal completely.
Place packets on a large, rimmed baking sheet, and roast 8-10 minutes for filets under an inch in thickness; 10-15 minutes for filets over 1 inch thick.
Transfer packets to plates. Slit tops with a knife, gently open.

Chef's note:
Try this flavor alternative:

Lemon Caper: omit basil. Add 3-4 lemon slices, and 4-5 capers per filet.

Bacon-Wrapped, Jalapeno and Cheese Stuffed Shrimp

Everything in moderation! Sometimes it's about the relationships with friends and family gathering for a good, fun meal, and a shot of tequila.

Makes: 4-6 servings

Ingredients
- 2 pounds large shrimp (U-16, approximately 16 per pound,) peeled, deveined, and rinsed
- 2 teaspoons smoked paprika
- 2 teaspoons sweet paprika
- 2 teaspoons cumin
- ½ teaspoon salt
- 8 ounces queso fresco
- 4 jalapenos, halved, seeded, and minced
- 1 pound bacon strips (thin cut,) cut in half
- ¼ cup raw honey
- 2 limes, 1 juiced, 1 wedged
- 3-4 habaneros (optional)
- wooden skewers, soaked in water

Directions
In a large bowl, mix together cumin, paprika, and salt. Add shrimp and toss to evenly coat.
In a bowl, crumble queso fresco, and mix in minced jalapenos.
Working with one shrimp at a time, press about 1 teaspoon of the queso fresco and jalapeno mix on the shrimp, then wrap base of shrimp all the way around with ½ slice of bacon. Repeat with rest of shrimp.
Thread shrimp onto skewers, 4 per skewer.
If you like heat, try habaneros on about ½ pound of the shrimp. Mix the habaneros in with the queso fresco, wrap and skewer, as above.
In a small jar, combine honey, and 2 tablespoons of lime juice. Shake to mix.
Preheat grill. Grill shrimp over high heat until bacon crisps, and shrimp is just cooked through, about 2-3 minutes per side.
Remove to a platter, and drizzle with honey lime. Serve with lime wedges.

Chef's note:
Can also be made with chicken tenders, if anyone in your family does not eat shrimp.

9

QUICK BITES

Maple Chai Ginger Trail Mix	93
Quesadilla	94
Cuban Sandwich	95
Protein Balls	96
Nachos	97

Nachos

Maple Chia Ginger Trail Mix

Maple Chai Ginger Trail Mix

This makes a great high protein snack, and is really yummy with yogurt for breakfast, or panna cotta for dessert. The addition of the traditional warming spices (ginger, cinnamon, cardamom, etc…) help aid digestion, and balance blood sugar. A study published in the *Diabetes Care Journal* found that cinnamon helps improve blood glucose, and cholesterol levels when consumed on a regular basis.

Makes: 4-6 servings

Ingredients
- 1½ cups raw almonds, slivered
- 1½ cups raw pumpkin seeds
- 1½ cups raw sunflower seeds
- ½ cup golden flax seeds
- ¾ cup dried blueberries
- ¾ cup crystalized ginger, diced
- ⅓ cup pure maple syrup
- ½ teaspoon kosher salt
- 1 teaspoon vanilla extract
- 2 tablespoons Chai Spice Mix

Chai Spice Mix
- 2 tablespoons ground cinnamon
- 2 tablespoons ground cardamom
- 2 teaspoons ground ginger
- 2 teaspoons Chinese five-spice powder
- 1 large nutmeg, grated
- 1 teaspoon fresh ground black pepper

Directions
Preheat the oven to 325°F.
Line a baking sheet with parchment paper.
In a small bowl, mix chai spice mix ingredients together.
In a large bowl, mix almonds, pumpkin seeds, sunflower seeds, and flaxseeds.
Add salt, chai spice mix, vanilla extract, and maple syrup. Stir to coat.
Pour seeds and almonds on prepared baking sheet. Bake for 40-45 minutes. The seeds and almonds should be a deep golden brown, and caramelized.
Remove from the oven, and allow to cool on the baking sheet. Once cool, mix in the crystalized ginger and blueberries.

Quesadilla

These are incredibly delicious and easy. A simple swap of ingredients can make them perfect for breakfast, lunch, or dinner. Running short on time? Quesadillas can be made faster than picking up a pizza, and are better for you.

Makes: 4 servings

Ingredients
- 8 flour tortillas, gordita size (8-inch)
- 2 leftover chicken breasts, sliced or leftover steak, sliced
- 4-6 baby bella, or shiitake mushrooms, sliced
- 1 red bell pepper, sliced
- 1 medium onion, chopped
- 1 cup spinach, chopped
- 4-5 ounces cheddar cheese, shredded
- 1 tablespoon unsalted butter

Directions
In a large sauté pan, over medium heat, melt ½ tablespoon of butter.
Add peppers, onions, and mushrooms. Cook until translucent, about 5 minutes. Add spinach, and sauté an additional 2 minutes.
Remove vegetable mixture, and set aside.
Heat up a skillet, and add touch of butter to coat pan.
Place tortilla in bottom of pan; place ¼ of the vegetable mixture, chicken, and cheese, then top with second tortilla.
Allow to cook for 3 minutes, flip, and cook for an additional 2 minutes.
Repeat for remaining quesadillas.
Cut each quesadilla into quarters, and serve warm.

Chef's Note:
Quesadillas are a great way to use leftover ingredients. If substituting, make sure ingredients are cooked before adding them to the quesadilla.

Cuban Sandwich

This is an excellent way to use leftover pork tenderloin, and makes a great quick lunch, or dinner. Naturally fermented dill pickles contain probiotics that help digestion of food, and aid in overall health.

Makes: 4 servings

Ingredients
- Leftover Prosciutto & Rosemary Wrapped Pork Tenderloin (page 78)
- 4 Italian sub rolls/ hoagie rolls
- 4 slices prosciutto
- 8 slices Swiss cheese
- 8 sandwich sliced dill pickles (recommended Bubbies pickles)
- Dijon mustard
- 2 tablespoons butter, softened

Directions
Preheat large griddle pan, or panni press.
Slice pork tenderloin in ¼ inch slices, 5-6 slices per sandwich.
Slice sub rolls and spread with mustard.
Cut Swiss cheese slices in half. Place 2 half slices of on top of the mustard, so entire sub roll has cheese. It will overlap some.
Add slices of pork on top of the Swiss cheese.
Top with 1 slice of prosciutto per sandwich.
Add 2 pickle slices per sandwich on top of the prosciutto.
Top pickles with 2 half slices of Swiss cheese.
Place on top of sub roll. Press sandwich down with your hands.
Reduce heat on griddle pan to low.
Butter top side of sandwich. Place sandwich, butter side down, onto griddle pan. Once all sandwiches are on your griddle pan, butter the bottom side of sandwich (which is now facing up.)
Cover sandwiches with a piece of foil, and, if using a griddle pan, set a cast iron pan or other heavy skillet on top of foil, to press your sandwich.
Cook for 5-6 minutes per side on low temperature, to allow pork to heat and cheese to melt.

Protein Balls

A healthy snack, or on-the-go breakfast. Protein Balls are packed with not only protein, but good fats, and nutrients to support heart and joint health. These are also great as a post workout snack.

Makes: 4-6 servings

Ingredients
- 1½ cups rolled oats
- ¼ cup hemp seeds
- ¼ cup chia seeds
- ½ cup cashews, chopped
- ¾ cup dark chocolate, chopped
- ½ cup peanut butter
- ⅓ cup pure maple syrup

Directions
Combine all ingredients in a large bowl.
Place mixture in the refrigerator for at least 10 minutes, to let mixture harden.
Take mixture out and roll ingredients into balls, working quickly.
Place balls in container, and set in fridge for at least 30 minutes to set.
Keep refrigerated.
Snack as needed.

Nachos

Many times we think of nachos simply as over salted corn chips, drowning in processed cheese. Nachos can be a healthier option, if you are loading up on veggies, and not too much cheese and sour cream. You will have crunch from the tortilla chips and lettuce, along with the radishes. The corn and peppers will give you a hint of sweetness. A great option for busy families, picky eaters, or family members with different dietary requirements.

Makes: 4-6 servings

Ingredients
- 1-2 pounds pork from the slow cooked carnitas recipe (page 79)
- tortilla chips

Directions
Reheat pork in a pan over medium heat. If needed, add a little water to keep pork from drying out.
To keep lettuce crisp, soak in ice water, then drain well, and dry in a salad spinner before using. Top tortilla chips with your favorite ingredients. We recommend topping individually this way we focus on quality rather than quantity.

Serve with:
- shredded romaine lettuce
- grilled corn
- radishes
- guacamole
- queso fresco, or shredded cheddar
- red peppers, diced
- olives
- jalapenos
- salsa

Chef's note:
The best thing about pork carnitas (page 79) is the recipe makes a lot, and it freezes very well. Freeze in smaller portions, and pull out what you need for dinner. If the pork is still frozen when you are reheating, add a couple of tablespoons of water to keep it from drying out. The water will evaporate as it continues to thaw and heat up.

10

SAUCES

Lemon Pesto	100
Sunday Gravy	101
Chimichurri	102
Romesco	103

Top to bottom: Lemon Pesto, Chimichurri, Romesco, Sunday Gravy

Lemon Pesto

Naturally detoxifying due to the lemon, parsley and basil, this is a perfect, tasty, and healthy dipping sauce. We keep a jar in our fridges at all times, for dipping veggies, or topping grilled chicken. Using almonds instead of pine nuts provides a great source of omega-3 fatty acids, and good-quality protein. Our favorite way to enjoy this is along with grilled green beans, better than french fries!

Makes: 1½ cups

Ingredients
- 1 cup fresh basil, packed
- ½ cup fresh parsley, packed
- ⅓ cup almonds, toasted
- 2 lemons, zested, and juiced
- ½ cup Parmigiano Reggiano cheese, grated
- 5 tablespoons extra-virgin olive oil
- 1 cloves garlic
- ¼ teaspoon kosher salt
- ¼ teaspoon fresh ground black pepper

Directions
Puree all ingredients in food processor or blender. Taste, and adjust salt and pepper as desired. Serve with grilled green beans, additional grilled vegetables, or grilled chicken.

Sunday Gravy

Sunday Gravy is essentially tomato sauce simmered all day with meat, or roasted bones. It is often made on Sundays in Italian families, which is how it got its name. Roasting bones allows the additional nutrients such as glucosamine, chondroitin, and gelatin to enter the sauce. A slow simmer allows nutrients that would cook off at a higher heat to stay within the sauce. This goes great over pasta, zucchini noodles, or with a slice of homemade bread.

Makes: 12 cups

Ingredients
- 4 -28 ounce cans crushed or diced tomatoes
- 1 white or yellow onion, grated
- 3 cloves garlic, crushed
- 1 teaspoon kosher salt
- 1 teaspoon fresh ground black pepper
- 1 tablespoon dried oregano
- 1 tablespoon dried parsley
- ½ teaspoon dried basil
- 1 teaspoon dried thyme
- 1½ to 2 pounds of soup bones, pork or beef
- 1 tablespoon balsamic vinegar (for deglazing the pan, optional)

Directions
Preheat oven to 425°F.
Season bones with ½ teaspoon salt and ½ teaspoon pepper. Place on baking sheet, or large cast-iron pan, and put in oven for 30 minutes to roast.
Combine all remaining ingredients in slow-cooker (6-7 quart,) or large sauce pot (see Chef's note below.)
Once bones are done roasting, remove from pan, and place into slow-cooker. Quickly deglaze the pan with balsamic vinegar, and pour into the slow-cooker for added flavor, if desired.
Cook on low for 8-10 hours. Turn the lid 90 degrees for the last two hours, to allow the liquid to reduce.

Chef's note:
If using a large sauce pot on a stove: Cook on low heat for 6 hours, lid on for the first 4 hours. Uncover for the last 2 hours, to allow the liquid to reduce. Be mindful of potential splatter with the lid off, should your sauce pot not be very deep.

Chimichurri

Parsley is a great detoxifier for the liver and kidneys. With the addition of the fat from the olive oil, it allows the body to utilize nutrients more efficiently. Chimichurri historically pairs very well with steaks, chicken, and seafood. It is especially great paired with Grilled Tri-Tip (page 83.)

Makes: 2½ cups

Ingredients
- 2 cups packed fresh Italian parsley
- 4 medium garlic cloves
- ¼ cup packed fresh oregano
- ¼ cup red wine vinegar
- 1 lemon, zested
- ½ teaspoon red pepper flakes
- ½ teaspoon kosher salt
- ½ teaspoon fresh ground black pepper
- 1 cup extra-virgin olive oil

Directions
Puree all ingredients in food processor, or blender. Taste, adjust salt and pepper, as desired.
Transfer sauce to an airtight container, and refrigerate at least 2 hours, and up to 1 day, to allow the flavors to meld.
Before serving, stir. Chimichurri will keep in the refrigerator for up to 1 week.

Romesco

Packed with protein and veggies, romesco is a fantastic, nutrient dense, sauce. Roasted peppers are high in vitamin A and C, which help your body to repair after injury, and keep the immune system healthy.

Makes: 2½ cups

Ingredients
- 2 red bell peppers, roasted, peeled, and seeded
- 2 medium tomatoes
- 3 cloves garlic
- 1 ancho chili, soaked in boiling water until soft (about 3 minutes,) stemmed, seeded
- 3 tablespoons raw hazelnuts
- 2 tablespoons raw almonds
- 1-2 teaspoons crushed red pepper flakes
- 1 slice of bread, torn into pieces
- 1 tablespoon red wine vinegar
- 5 tablespoons extra-virgin olive oil
- kosher salt, to taste
- fresh ground black pepper, to taste

Directions

Preheat oven to 375°F.
Place tomatoes and garlic onto a baking sheet. Drizzle with 1 tablespoon olive oil, and put in oven.
Roast for 30 minutes until garlic is soft, and tomato skin has blistered.
Remove from oven, take skin from garlic, and peel tomatoes.
Meanwhile, heat 1 tablespoon of olive oil in a skillet, over medium heat. Add almonds and hazelnuts. Sauté until lightly toasted, about 1 minute.
Using a slotted spoon, add nuts to food processor or blender.
Add torn bread to skillet, cook until toasted. Add to food processor.
Transfer tomatoes, garlic, red bell pepper, ancho chili, and vinegar, to food processor.
Pulse several times to a course puree. Season with crushed red pepper, salt, and pepper. Slowly incorporate remaining olive oil while pulsing the food processor.

11

SWEET INDULGENCES

Lemon Bars	107
Rhubarb & Strawberry Ice Pops	108
Blueberry Crisp	109
Fudgy Brownies	110
Blackberry & Ginger Ice cream	111
Lavender & Lemon Panna Cotta	112
Blueberry & Ginger Cookies	113

Lavender & Lemon Panna Cotta

Lemon Bars

Lemon Bars

There are just some desserts that need to be sinful, and this is one of them. To get a good, solid, lemon flavor, you need a lot of lemon. To balance the tartness, however, you need sugar. Loaded with sugar, butter, and fresh lemons, they're delicious, but definitely a recipe to be shared.

Makes: 20 bars

Ingredients

For the crust:
- ½ pound unsalted butter (2 sticks,) at room temperature
- ½ cup granulated sugar
- 2 cups all-purpose flour
- pinch of kosher salt

For the filling:
- 7 large eggs at room temperature
- 3 cups granulated sugar
- 6 lemons, zested, 1 cup juice
- 1 cup all-purpose flour
- 1 teaspoon fresh ginger, grated
- powdered sugar, for garnish

Directions

Preheat the oven to 350°F.
For the crust, cream the butter and sugar until light, using an electric mixer fitted with a paddle attachment.
Combine the flour and salt, and with the mixer on low, add to the butter until just mixed.
Flatten the dough with floured hands. Press it into a 9x13x2-inch baking pan, building up a ½ - inch edge on all sides. Chill for 15 minutes.
Bake the crust for 15-20 minutes, until very lightly browned. Let cool on a wire rack. Leave the oven on at 350°F.
For the filling, whisk together the eggs, sugar, lemon zest, lemon juice, and flour. Pour over the crust, and bake for 30-35 minutes until the filling is set. Let cool to room temperature.
Cut into squares, and dust with powdered sugar.

Rhubarb & Strawberry Ice Pops

Rhubarb is a good source of calcium, which aids in healthy teeth and bones. It contains Lutein, which is great for the health of skin and eyes. The addition of strawberries provides vitamin C, which boosts the immune system. These pops are great for kids and they have a lot of color, making them not only healthy, but fun.

Makes: 4 ice pops

Ingredients
Rhubarb & Strawberry Layer
- ¼ cup raw honey
- 1 cup strawberries
- 1 cup rhubarb
- 1 teaspoon vanilla extract

Coconut Layer
- 1 can coconut milk (full fat)
- 2 tablespoons raw honey
- ¼ teaspoon vanilla extract

Directions
Combine all ingredients for the rhubarb and strawberry layer in a pan. Simmer until fruit is soft, about 3-5 minutes.
Place fruit mixture in blender, and blend until smooth.
Cool to room temperature.
In a separate bowl, mix coconut layer ingredients.
Pour fruit mixture and coconut mixture into ice pop molds, alternating layers.
Freeze 4 hours, or until firm.

Blueberry Crisp

Blueberries are high in an antioxidant called anthocyanin (it's what gives them their blue color,) which have been found to reduce the risk of heart disease. This recipe can easily be altered to fit seasonal fruit, such as cherries, pears, peaches, or apples.

Makes: 4-6 servings

Ingredients
- 4 cups fresh or frozen blueberries
- 1 lemon, zested, 1 tablespoon juice
- 2 tablespoons orange juice
- 1 teaspoon vanilla
- ½ teaspoon fresh ginger, grated
- 2 tablespoons all-purpose flour
- Vanilla bean ice cream, for serving (optional)

Topping
- ¾ cup firmly packed light brown sugar
- ½ cup all-purpose flour
- ½ teaspoon ground cinnamon
- 4 tablespoons unsalted butter, room temperature
- ¾ cup rolled oats
- 1 pinch of kosher salt

Directions
Preheat an oven to 375°F.
Grease a 1½-quart baking dish with butter.
In a bowl, sprinkle flour over blueberries. Add lemon zest, orange, lemon juice, and ginger. Spread blueberries evenly over the bottom of the buttered baking dish.
In a bowl, using a pastry blender or fork, mix together the brown sugar, flour, cinnamon, butter, salt, and rolled oats, until well combined. Sprinkle evenly over the blueberries.
Bake until the top is golden, and the blueberries are bubbling, about 30 minutes. Transfer to a wire rack and let cool for a few minutes. Serve hot or warm, with vanilla bean ice cream.

Chef's note:
For other seasonal fruits, simply replace the blueberries with an equal amount of that seasonal fruit.

Fudgy Brownies

Raw cacao powder is similar to cocoa powder, but less processed. It still contains the vitamins and minerals that are missing in the cocoa powder. Raw cacao contains magnesium, which is helpful for metabolism, and electrolyte balance.

Makes: 16 brownies

Ingredients
- 10 tablespoons unsalted butter
- 1¼ cups granulated sugar
- ¾ cup plus 2 tablespoons raw cacao powder
- ¼ rounded teaspoon kosher salt
- 1 teaspoon vanilla extract
- 2 large eggs
- ½ cup all-purpose flour
- ½ cup chopped bittersweet chocolate (60% cacao)
- ½ cup chopped walnuts or pecans (optional)

Directions
Preheat oven to 325°F.
Line the bottom and sides of an 8-inch square baking pan with parchment paper, leaving an overhang off the edges of the pan. (This helps when removing the baked brownies from the pan.)
Add water to a medium saucepan, 1-2 inches deep. Heat water until barely simmering. Combine butter, sugar, cocoa powder, and salt, in a glass or metal (heat safe) bowl. Rest bowl over simmering water (if the bottom of the bowl touches the water, remove a little water.)
Stir mixture occasionally until the butter has melted, and mixture is quite warm. Don't worry if it looks gritty, it will become smooth once you add the eggs and flour.
Remove the bowl from heat, and set aside until only warm, about 3-5 minutes.
Stir in vanilla with a wooden spoon or spatula. Add eggs, one at a time, stirring vigorously after each one.
When the batter looks thick, shiny, and well blended, add the flour. Stir until fully incorporated, then beat with the wooden spoon or spatula for 40-50 strokes. (The batter will be quite thick.) Fold in chopped chocolate (and nuts, if using.) Spread evenly in lined pan.
Bake 25-28 minutes, or until a toothpick can be inserted into the center and come out almost clean (you want the toothpick to be a little moist with batter.)
Cool completely, then remove from pan. For the cleanest lines when cutting, place into freezer for 20-30 minutes to firm up. Cut into 16 squares.

Chef's note:
Unsweetened cocoa powder can be used, but it will not have the health benefits of the raw cacao powder.

Blackberry Ginger Ice Cream

Ice cream is a such a great summertime treat, and the availability of fresh berries makes it even better. If we are going to indulge in something, wouldn't it make sense to enjoy something truly delicious? When making homemade ice cream, you have the ability to control the ingredients, such as using farm fresh raw milk. Since raw milk has not been heated, the enzymes needed to break down the milk are still present. Many people intolerant to pasteurized milk find that they are able to enjoy raw milk, as the enzymes are still intact.

Makes: 1 ½ quarts
Requires: Ice cream maker

Ingredients
- 2 cups whole milk
- 2 cups heavy cream
- 1 cup granulated sugar
- Pinch table salt
- ½ vanilla bean, halved, seeds scraped
- 5 large egg yolks
- 1½ inch piece of fresh ginger, peeled, sliced into 6-8 slices
- 1 teaspoon pure vanilla extract
- 2¼ cups blackberries fresh or frozen (thawed)
- 1 tablespoon granulated sugar

Directions
In a small bowl combine blackberries and 1 tablespoon sugar. Set aside, so berries macerate.
In a medium saucepan, set over medium-low heat, add the milk, cream, ½ cup of the sugar, salt, ginger, and the scraped vanilla bean (including the pod.)
Whisk to combine, and bring the mixture to a slight boil.
While the milk & cream mixture is heating, combine the yolks and ½ cup of sugar in a medium bowl. Using a hand mixer on low speed, or a whisk, beat until mixture is pale and thick.
Once the milk & cream mixture has come to a slight boil, whisk about ¼ of it into the yolk & sugar mixture.
Whisk in another ½ of the milk & cream mixture to the yolk & sugar mixture. Then return the combined mixture to the saucepan, along with the remaining milk & cream mixture.
Using a wooden spoon, stir the mixture constantly over low heat, until it thickens slightly, and coats the back of the spoon. This mixture must NOT boil or the yolks will overcook – the process should only take a few minutes.
Pour the mixture through a fine mesh strainer, and discard the vanilla pod.
In a food processor, or blender, puree the blackberries. Pour blackberries through fine mesh strainer, and combine with ice cream mixture.
Stir in vanilla extract.
Bring ice cream mixture to room temperature, cover, and refrigerate 1-2 hours, or overnight.
Follow manufacturer's instructions specific to your ice cream maker for freezing the ice cream.

Lavender & Lemon Panna Cotta

This is a simple, easy dessert. Lavender is often thought of as a flower, but it is actually an edible herb, most commonly seen in baked goods. While too much lavender can often lend a perfume like taste, just a little bit gives a light, clean flavor. Combined with lemon, it makes a wonderful panna cotta.

Makes: 4 servings

Ingredients
- 2 cups heavy cream
- 1½ teaspoons gelatin
- 1 lemon, 1 teaspoon zested, 1 tablespoon juice
- ¾ teaspoon fresh lavender, chopped
- ¼ cup pure maple syrup

Directions
In a bowl, combine 1 cup of cream with gelatin, to allow gelatin to bloom (gelatin absorbs all liquid.)
Once bloomed, place gelatin and remaining cream in saucepan over low heat, until gelatin is fully dissolved. Do not boil.
Remove from heat. Combine with lemon juice, lavender, lemon zest, and maple syrup.
Pour mixture into ramekins. Refrigerate until firm, about 4 hours.

Dietary Alternatives
Dairy-free: substitute coconut milk for heavy cream.

Blueberry Ginger Cookies

There is always something very comforting about a cookie. Who doesn't have a favorite cookie? You might have a new one after trying these! We love the crunchy ends of cookies, and this cookie is one big crunchy end. Its full of flavor, from the sweetness of the blueberries, to the spice of the crystalized ginger.

Makes: 36 cookies

Ingredients
- 2 cups all-purpose flour
- 1 teaspoon baking soda
- 2 teaspoons salt
- 1 cup unsalted butter, (2 sticks)
- ¾ cup granulated sugar, (reserve 1 tablespoon)
- ¾ cup dark brown sugar, firmly packed
- 1 teaspoon water
- 1 teaspoon vanilla
- 2 large eggs
- 1 cup dried blueberries
- 1 cup crystalized ginger, diced

Directions
Preheat oven to 350°F.
Line 2-3 cookie sheets with parchment paper.
Dice crystalized ginger, then in a small bowl, mix with the 1 tablespoon of reserved sugar, to prevent from sticking together.
In a large bowl, combine flour, baking soda, salt, and stir together.
In another large bowl, cream the butter and both sugars, then add the water and vanilla. Mix until just combined.
Add eggs, one at a time, to the butter mixture, and mix them lightly.
Stir in the flour mixture. When flour is mixed in, fold in the blueberries and ginger.
Using a 1 ounce scoop, drop cookie dough 2-inches apart onto prepared cookie sheets, approximately 6 cookies per tray. Cookies will spread during baking.
Bake for 13-17 minutes, or until the edges and centers of the cookies are golden brown.
Remove from oven, and allow cookies to cool on wire racks.

GLUTEN-FREE INDEX

While many of our recipes have gluten-free alternatives, this is a list of those which are gluten-free, as listed.

Brunch
Chia Seed Pudding, 25
Spinach and Mushroom Frittata, 27
Fruit Kabobs 29

Pasta & Grains
Moroccan Inspired Couscous, 39
Soba Noodle Salad *,40
Cherry Pistachio Quinoa Salad, 41

Vegetables
Grilled Green Beans, 46
Fennel, Carrot & Apple Salad, 48
Grilled Orange Sugar Snap Peas, 49
Apple & Shaved Brussels Sprouts Salad, 50
Spicy Cauliflower*,51
Extra Crispy Potatoes,52
Maple Roasted Delicata Squash, 53
Roasted Butternut with Grapes, 54
Zucchini Pasta, 55
Roasted Broccoli & Lemon, 56
Lemony Potato Salad, 57
Kale & Peach Salad, 58
Kale Chips, 59

Soup
Bone Broth, 62
Sausage & Lentil Soup*, 63
Oxtail Stew, 65
Roasted Tomato Basil Soup, 66

Poultry
Chicken Thighs Fennel & Oranges, 70
Five-Spice & Ginger Grilled Chicken, 71
Honey Lime Grilled Chicken Breast, 72
Roasted Duck, 73
Bourbon Maple Chicken Legs, 74

Meat
Prosciutto Wrapped Pork Tenderloin*, 78
Slow-cooker Carnitas, 79
Braised Short Ribs*, 79
Pork Shoulder & Ginger Beer, 80
Hearty Beef Stew, 82
Grilled Tri-Tip, 83

Seafood
Salmon Caramelized Onions & Apples, 86
Seared Scallops, 87
Cod en Papillote with Asparagus, 88
Bacon Jalapeno Cheese Stuffed Shrimp, 89

Quick Bites
Maple Chai Ginger Trail Mix, 93
Protein Balls*, 96
Nachos *, 97

Sauces
Lemon Pesto, 100
Sunday Gravy, 101
Chimichurri, 102
Romesco, 103

Sweet Indulgence
Rhubarb & Strawberry Ice Pops, 108
Blackberry Ginger Ice-cream, 111
Lavender & Lemon Panna Cotta, 112

*Not all brands of ingredients for these dishes are gluten-free. Please read labels carefully to ensure what you buy is gluten-free.

PANTRY LIST
Common items to keep on hand

- Seasonal fruits
- Seasonal vegetables
- Extra-virgin olive oil
- Unsalted butter
- Coconut oil
- Coconut milk
- Parmigiano Reggiano cheese
- Head of garlic
- Onions
- All-purpose flour
- Rice flour or gluten-free all-purpose flour
- Dried pasta
- Soba or rice noodles
- Dijon mustard
- Rice vinegar
- Apple cider vinegar
- Lemons
- Kosher & Himalayan salt
- Whole peppercorns
- Raw Honey
- Pure Maple Syrup
- Panko
- Assortment of fresh seasonal herbs (oregano, basil, parsley, thyme, rosemary)
- Assortment of dried herbs (ginger, cumin, turmeric, cinnamon, cardamom, nutmeg)

COMMON LIST OF SUBSTITUTIONS

There are times in the middle of a recipe we realize we are missing and ingredient, this list is helpful during those times.

Ingredient	Amount	Substitute
Buttermilk	1 cup	1 tablespoon vinegar or lemon juice + enough milk to make 1 cup (allow to sit for 10 minutes.)
Sour cream	1 cup	1 cup plain Greek yogurt
Oil	1 cup	1 cup applesauce
		1 cup coconut oil, melted
		1 cup butter melted
Egg	1 large	1 tablespoon ground chia or flax seeds + 3 tablespoons water (blend until mixture is thick and egg-like. Mixture may need to sit for a few minutes.)
		¼ cup unsweetened applesauce
Milk	1 cup	1 cup coconut milk
Cornstarch	1 tablespoon	1 tablespoon potato starch or arrowroot

ABOUT THE AUTHORS

Laura Timbrook CHC, AADP, is a certified Integrative Nutrition Coach, and wellness speaker. Her approach to quality nutrition is based on balance and simplicity, not on those that require immense willpower and "restrictions." She shares her love of the outdoors, crossfit, and '68 Mustangs, with her husband, three kids, and Blue, their Siberian Husky & Malamute mix rescue.

www.lauratimbrook.com

Paige Hansen holds an Associate's Degree in Culinary Arts from Sullivan University. She has spent several years in the restaurant and hospitality industry, both in the kitchen and management. She shares her love of food, red wine, yoga, and rescue animals, with her husband, along with Zoey, a Catahoula mix rescue, and Piper, a Australian Shepherd mix rescue.

www.verdegoodeats.com

Made in the USA
Middletown, DE
22 April 2021